T0079736

PORK

Edible

Series Editor: Andrew F. Smith

EDIBLE is a revolutionary new series of books dedicated to food and drink that explores the rich history of cuisine. Each book reveals the global history and culture of one type of food or beverage.

Already published

Apple Erika Janik

Bread William Rubel

Cake Nicola Humble

Caviar Nichola Fletcher

Champagne Becky Sue Epstein

Cheese Andrew Dalby

Chocolate Sarah Moss and
Alexander Badenoch

Cocktails Joseph M. Carlin

Curry Colleen Taylor Sen

Dates Nawal Nasrallah

Gin Lesley Jacobs Solmonson

Hamburger Andrew F. Smith

Herbs Gary Allen

Hot Dog Bruce Kraig

Ice Cream Laura B. Weiss

Lemon Toby Sonneman

Lobster Elisabeth Townsend

Milk Hannah Velten

Olive Fabrizia Lanza

Pancake Ken Albala

Pie Janet Clarkson

Pizza Carol Helstosky

Potato Andrew F. Smith

Pudding Jeri Quinzio

Rum Richard Foss

Sandwich Bee Wilson

Soup Janet Clarkson

Spices Fred Czarra

Tea Helen Saberi

Vodka Patricia Herlihy

Whiskey Kevin R. Kosar

Pork

A Global History

Katharine M. Rogers

REAKTION BOOKS

Published by Reaktion Books Ltd
33 Great Sutton Street
London EC1V 0DX, UK
www.reaktionbooks.co.uk

First published 2012

Copyright © Katharine M. Rogers 2012

All rights reserved
No part of this publication may be reproduced, stored in a retrieval
system, or transmitted, in any form or by any means, electronic,
mechanical, photocopying, recording or otherwise, without the prior
permission of the publishers.

Printed and bound in China by Eurasia

British Library Cataloguing in Publication Data
Rogers, Katharine M.
Pork : a global history. – (Edible)
1. Pork. 2. Cooking (Pork) – History. 3. Cooking (Pork)
I. Title II. Series
641.3´64-DC23

ISBN 978 1 78023 040 5

Contents

I
The Ideal Meat Producer

About 7,000 years ago, people in the Near East and perhaps also in China domesticated *Sus scrofa*, the Eurasian wild boar. Since then, pigs have provided the most widely eaten meat in the world. Pork is the most versatile of meats – ranging from the rich, delicate succulence of a roast loin to the dry, salty assertiveness of ham and bacon. Charles Lamb celebrated the delights of roast suckling pig, particularly its crisp skin, in his 'Dissertation on Upon Roast Pig' (1823): 'Crisp, tawny, well-watched, not over-roasted, *crackling*' offers 'the pleasure of overcoming the coy, brittle resistance' of browned skin together with the 'indefinable sweetness' of the meltingly tender fat layer underneath, 'the cream and quintessence of the child-pig's yet pure food . . . fat and lean . . . so blended and running into each other, that both together make but one ambrosian result, or common substance.'[1] Jane and Michael Stern describe the huge, one-pound grilled Iowa pork chop sold at the Pork Tent at the Iowa State Fair, the proud centre of pork raising in the usa. Though the chop is over an inch thick, it is so tender that it can be cut with a flimsy plastic knife: 'No other meat we know, white or red, has such fathomless succulence.'[2] Sara Perry could rely on general agreement when she titled a cookbook *Everything Tastes Better with Bacon*.

John Frederick Herring Sr (1795–1865), *A Family of Pigs*, oil on canvas.

Although a roast suckling pig is the most luxurious form of pork, almost every part of a pig is edible, including its blood (black pudding) and tail (flavouring for soups and stews). Jane Grigson, writing in 1967, deplored the distaste of the English for the less obviously promising parts of a pig, and expanded on what could be done:

> The skilful and economical housewife can buy a pig's head for 3/ or 4/; this is what she can make from it – pig's ears with a piquant sauce . . . brains in puff pastry . . . Bath chap [the cheek, cured, smoked, and simmered – something like a small ham] . . . 1½ pounds of sausage meat for making *pâté* or [sausages] . . . There is an average of 4½ pounds of boneless meat on a pig's head. And an excellent clear soup . . . or aspic jelly . . . is to be made of the bones.[3]

Even pig's bladder can be highly desirable. Guinea-hen-in-pig-bladder was a popular dish at a two-Michelin-star restaurant in Las Vegas until the authorities forced them to remove it because they were getting the bladders from an unapproved source. So far they have been unable to locate an approved one, because American meat packers routinely grind up the bladders for dog food.

Pig fat – lard – was for centuries the most common fat for frying and for shortening cakes and pastry in northern Europe and America. It was rendered at home and could be kept for many months in the cool, aptly named larder. It is less used now, because of the availability of butter and oil and our awareness of the dangers of saturated fat, in which lard is particularly rich. Lard was also used as a preservative: covering meat with a layer of lard kept it from contact with the air. When some meat was needed, the fat was melted, the necessary meat taken out, and the crock replaced in a cool larder to re-solidify.

Pork should be greyish pink and covered with a layer of firm white fat; it is the fat that makes it so tasty and succulent.

German *schmalz* or lard.

Nevertheless, mindful of current concerns about health, American and European breeders are now producing leaner pigs. They now average 16 per cent leaner with 27 per cent less saturated fat than they had nineteen years ago. The United States National Pork Board is calling pork 'the other white meat' in hopes of persuading people to see it as a low-fat and low-cholesterol alternative to turkey and chicken. The Board has found a study that shows pork 'supports weight loss goals', as well as being full of minerals and vitamins. On the other hand, many Chinese and other cooks deplore this sacrifice of flavour to a healthful diet.

Salting, drying and smoking were invented in order to preserve meat in the days before refrigeration, when it was essential to find a way to make use of all of an animal's meat long after it had been slaughtered. Salt draws water out of meat cells, and dehydration kills bacteria or inhibits them

Attributed to James Clark, *Three Prize Pigs in a Pen*, c. 1865, oil on canvas. These 19th-century animals show the older ideal for pigs.

Local government inspectors examining the carcasses of pigs, 1954.

from multiplying. Smoking helps the slow drying process and gives additional flavour. In the case of pork, more than other meats, these processes create products that are delicious in their own right. Not only does the high fat content of pork allow it to retain some succulence even after smoking, but drying and smoking might be said to improve pork by firming its texture and intensifying its flavour. Corned or jerked beef are not nearly so flavoursome as bacon, ham or cured sausage.

Paul Gauguin, *The Ham*, 1889, oil on canvas. A traditionally cured ham.

Today, about 30 per cent of the flesh from a pig is cooked fresh, as roasts or chops; the rest is cured for bacon and ham, ground up for sausage, or rendered into lard. Hams and shoulders are first salted, either with dry salt or brine, with a small amount of saltpeter (nitrate) added. After a period from a few days to several months, the meat is removed from the salt and dried, sometimes simply by hanging it in cool air. Usually it is smoked, often over a fire burning a particular wood, such as oak, hickory or pine. Nowadays ordinary hams are quickly cured by injection with a brine of salt, other sodium compounds and sugar, aged at room temperature for one week, and smoked for six to 48 hours. They are consequently relatively soft, mild-flavoured and perishable. In addition they are often precooked; that is, heated to an internal temperature

MORRIS

Baked ham! It looks awfully good, doesn't it? But it's the taste that tells. Looks don't prove much about food: not even with experts.

That's why we cure these hams "just so." Only *one* cure passes our *Supreme* Test and gives the exquisite, mild flavor we mark Morris *Supreme*. When you've tasted this ham we think you'll agree we've named it right.

There are many other Morris foods that bear this same mark of *Supreme* goodness. Bacon, sausage, lard; meats, fruits and vegetables in cans. You'll like them all.

MORRIS & COMPANY

Morris's Baked Ham poster, 1919. The type of ham on sale in supermarkets today.

One of the world's finest hams, Bayonne ham is painstakingly cured and aged for months.

of 155°F/68°C. Such 'fully cooked' hams can be served without further preparation.

Speciality hams are still made by traditional methods: rubbed all over with dry salt and then aged for months in a cool place. Bayonne and Parma hams are made by salting a hog's leg for a couple of weeks and hanging it to dry in a cool, humid cellar for months. Parma ham comes from Landrace or Duroc pigs fed on grain and whey (a by-product of making the local Parmesan cheese), which are killed at a minimum of nine months old and cured by slow air-drying for twelve months, during which the cut surfaces are constantly brushed with seasoned lard. The world's best hams are said to come from *ibérico* pigs in southwestern Spain. They are nourished almost entirely on acorns from a particular kind of evergreen oak tree, which they pick up roaming freely in the woods. Their hams must be cured for three years. Their meat is intense in flavour and infiltrated with particularly succulent fat, and it is very, very expensive – $130 a pound in the US. All these hams are served raw, usually as an appetizer. The country hams of Virginia, Tennessee, Kentucky and the Carolinas are salted, smoked in a constant cloud of aromatic smoke provided by a low fire of beechwood or hickory, and then hung to cure for a year. They are soaked and cooked before eating, as is Yunnan ham, the finest Chinese ham. Bacon is the fat meat of pork sides or (especially in the US) pork belly, processed in the same way. Properly prepared, ham and bacon can be kept for a full year. In addition to being enjoyed as meats in their own right, ham and bacon are invaluable for flavouring other dishes, from a poor person's pot of beans to a gourmet's *coq au vin*.

Sausages were invented to make use of the odd leftover bits of a pig – trimmings from choice cuts, inner organs, fat and blood; if sausages are dried or smoked, they too will keep for many months. Although any kind of meat can be turned into sausage, pork has been traditionally used and is most common because of the quality of its meat and fat. The latter is important because fat is necessary to keep sausages moist and tasty; most contain 20 to 30 per cent or even 50 per cent fat. They are highly seasoned with salt, pepper and various herbs and spices. Well-cleaned intestines (of pigs or other animals, depending on the size wanted) make a perfect cooking vessel for sausages – edible, light, strong, holding in meat and juices when fresh sausages are being browned,

Henry Le Monnier, *Saucissons le Lyonnais*, poster, 1930.

while letting moisture escape when they are to be dried for lengthy keeping. Sausages are economical because of their cheap ingredients, and at the same time delicious when well seasoned, moistened with tasty fat, and often smoked or dried to intensify their flavour, so they appeal to both poor and rich.

Every country has its distinctive sausages, from Italian salami to German *Leberwurst* to Chinese *lap cheung* to Mexican

'The Sausage Seller': a 'marchande de saucisses' sells her wares on the
streets of Paris, c. 1790.

chorizo to American breakfast sausages. Fresh sausage is made
by grinding pork meat and fat with seasonings and stuffing it
into casings; it is intended to be cooked promptly. The raw
meat in sausages that are to be kept for a long time, such as
salami, is mixed with salt, saltpeter and flavourings; after it is

A pig foraging in Rajasthan, India. Up until the 19th century, pigs roamed at large in Europe and America.

stuffed into casings, the sausages are dried, usually in cool moving air, but sometimes over heat. After several weeks of drying, the meat will have undergone fermentation by bacteria that generate lactic acid, which preserves it and gives it a tangy flavour. Finally the sausage may be smoked. Such sausages are safely eaten without cooking. A dependable dry wind is important for curing sausages, which means damp countries like England are at a disadvantage and have not developed cured sausages.

Pigs are easy to keep because they are omnivorous. They do not require extensive land for grazing like cows or sheep, but can forage on their own in woods or even in city streets, or be kept in small pens and live on human leavings. They can be fed whatever is cheap – sweet potatoes in New Guinea, corn (*Zea mays*) in the US Midwest, coconuts in Polynesia. Moreover, they breed and grow faster than cows or sheep. While a cow produces one calf after nine months, a pig produces ten piglets after four.

2

Prejudices Against the Pig

Despite its usefulness, the pig is the object of the best known of food taboos. It is the only commonly eaten animal that is widely regarded as unclean. Both Jews and Muslims are forbidden to eat pigs, most likely because they are scavengers. The Old Testament (Leviticus 11:7, Deuteronomy 14:8) declares swine to be unclean to Jews because, although they are cloven-footed, they do not chew the cud like cattle, sheep and goats. Chewing the cud, an adaptation for extracting maximum nutrition from plants, indicates an exclusively plant diet. Pigs, on the other hand, nourish themselves with almost anything they can get, including meat, tubers, garbage and even excrement. In former times, when they roamed at large in villages and cities, people would have been constantly reminded of their propensity to eat disgusting things.

While perceived filthy habits seems the obvious reason for people's distaste for eating pig, there are other causative factors. Mary Douglas attributes the ancient Hebrews' rejection of the pig to the fact that it does not fit into a proper, clearly defined class in their understanding of animal classification: animals with cloven hoofs, like cows, goats and sheep, should chew the cud because that indicates that they live on grass. Moreover, nomadic peoples like the early Hebrews (and Arabs) were used to keeping animals that can be moved in herds – cattle, sheep and goats – rather than pigs, which prefer to roam on their own around their home base. The nomads associated keeping pigs with the alien sedentary lifestyle they had rejected and reinforced this distaste with a religious prohibition; this remained in force even after they had settled down.

Once these food regulations were in place, they served to help define the Jews' identity as a separate people, sharply distinguished from the surrounding unbelievers. In the second century BCE, when the Greek Seleucid King Antiochus IV Epiphanes ruled Judea, he tried to Hellenize Jewish culture by forcing the Jews to violate their sacred laws, including the taboo on swine. Those who refused to sacrifice or eat swine were executed. Maintaining their special identity became even more urgent to Jews after the diaspora. They would have

Eleazar, an aged scribe, defied King Antiochus' order to eat pork. The king had him seized, tortured and executed.

found the pig more abhorrent than other unclean animals, such as shellfish, because pork and bacon were omnipresent all over Europe. The Jews' revulsion against the unclean pig doubtless became more intense as they were persecuted by the Gentile pig-relishing majority.

The Jewish philosopher Maimonides (1135–1204) rationalized the pork taboo partly on health grounds, declaring that pork was indigestible, but more forcefully on hygienic grounds: the pig's 'habits and its food are very dirty and loathsome'. If Jews were allowed to eat pork, their 'streets and houses would be more dirty than any cesspool, as may be seen at present in the country of the Franks'.[1] It is true that eating pork can be unhealthy because pigs carry trichinosis, but this connection could not have been made by the biblical writers or Maimonides: the disease and the parasite that causes it were not identified until the nineteenth century.

Modern consumers in the developed world are protected by government inspection of pork. In this early 20th-century photograph, USDA workers inspect pork samples for signs of trichinosis.

Art Young, 'Time to Butcher', political cartoon for the cover of *The Coming Nation*, 26 October 1912. Gentiles also tend to stereotype pigs negatively.

October 26, 1912   **THE**   Price 5 Cents

COMING NATION

A JOURNAL OF THINGS DOING AND TO BE DONE

Time to Butcher

For the sake of the beast itself as well as the people

When he first preached Islam, Muhammad would also have felt the need to unify his small band of followers with an identity reinforced by food taboos, which he found ready to hand in the Bible. His prohibitions, however, were more limited – forbidding only pig meat and blood, as well as animals that had not been purposely slaughtered for food and those that had been slaughtered for pagan sacrifice. The association of pork with uncleanliness and unhealthiness continues to this day. Muslim Uyghurs in China are revolted by the Chinese readiness to eat 'everything', and constantly worry about Chinese cooks polluting their food with pork. Food writer Fuchsia Dunlop's Uyghur taxi driver assured her that 'if a true

Muslim eats pork, his skin will erupt into blood-spouting boils that can be fatal'.[2]

It may also be that the biblical and Koranic prohibitions rationalized some prehistoric taboo on the pig among Middle Eastern tribes. Such a taboo presumably underlay the aversion to pork that prevailed in parts of Scotland through the eighteenth century and was noted by Samuel Johnson and Walter Scott. Blood puddings are generally made of pig's blood, but the Scottish version, haggis, is made of sheep's blood in a sheep's stomach.

Finally, pigs would not have been so delightfully easy to keep in the arid Middle East as in European woodlands. In damp, wooded areas, they find the shade and mud wallows they require because they are subject to sunburn and have no sweat glands, and they can feed themselves in forests filled with nuts.

3
Pork in Europe

In Homer's *Iliad* the hero Achilles entertains guests with 'the chine [loin] of a great hog rich in lard' (as well as the chines of a sheep and a goat); he and Patroclus cut up the meat, spit the pieces, salt them, and roast them over the embers of an open fire; then they serve the meat with bread and wine (Book IX). Cuisine gradually became more sophisticated, although we do not have detailed recipes until Roman times. However, ordinary Greeks had little access to prime roasting meat and were more familiar with sausages, including black puddings and sweetened sausages. In his satire *The Knights*, Aristophanes (*c.* 446 BCE– *c.* 386 BCE) compares a sausage seller to a politician because both trades involve mincing all policies together and dressing them up with sauce. Black puddings, typically made of pig's blood, were also made by the Assyrians and are found, in various versions, in many European countries. French black puddings, *boudins noirs*, may include fresh pork fat, onions, spices and cream and are often served after midnight mass on Christmas Eve. The famously horrible Spartan black broth was a stew of pork, barley, salt and vinegar.

Pork seems to have been the favourite meat of the Romans: it added a bit of flavour to a simple farm meal and formed the centrepiece of luxurious banquets. The Romans (like the Chinese) considered pork the most wholesome and digestible of meats. The Greek physician and philosopher Galen (AD 129–199), who practised in Rome, declared it 'the most nutritious of all foods'; people who did hard physical work, from athletes to ditch-diggers, became visibly weaker if they substituted a different food. He added that pig and human flesh are so similar in taste and smell that some people have unsuspectingly eaten human flesh under the impression that it was pork.[1] Pliny the Elder (AD 29–79) may have been the first to praise pork for the diversity of pleasures it provides: it offers 'almost fifty flavours, whereas all other meats have one each'.[2] In addition to the rich variety of cured pork products, fresh pork takes particularly well to a diverse range of spices and flavourings.

Anne Vallayer-Coster, *Still-life with Ham, Bottles and Radishes*, 1767, oil on canvas.

Trimalchio's feast, a still from Federico Fellini's *Satyricon* (1970).

Roman soldiers on the march carried rations of cured sausages. A speaker in Varro's *On Agriculture* (first century BCE) remarks that every Roman with a farm kept pigs. Horace's sturdy tenant-farmer neighbour, Ofellus, regularly ate greens and the shank of a smoked ham on working days, although he would serve company a pullet or a kid (Satire ii.2). Baucis and Philemon, the poverty-stricken cottagers who offered their best hospitality to the disguised gods Zeus and Hermes, gave them a dish of cabbage seasoned with one thin slice of pork.

At the same time, the numerous dishes served at every Roman feast regularly included pork, cooked in elaborate ways. It often took the form of a whole roast pig stuffed with exotic ingredients. The feast given by the vulgar freedman Trimalchio in Petronius' *Satyricon* merely exaggerates the ostentation of a typical Roman banquet. The most spectacular item is an enormous wild sow, adorned with the cap of a freed slave and surrounded by piglets made of pastry apparently sucking her teats; she is stuffed with live thrushes. Pigs figure throughout the dinner, which culminates in a stupid joke wherein the cook pretends to have forgotten to clean an even bigger pig, begs for forgiveness, and finally prepares to gut it on the spot; when he cuts it open, black puddings and sausages pour out. Athenaeus, an Egyptian Greek living in Rome, gives a colourful picture of luxurious late classical cuisine in his *Deipnosophists* ('Learned Dining-Club', second century CE). The gourmet conversationalists lovingly recall innumerable banquets featuring pork, as well as particular dishes such as boiled sow's uterus floating in vinegar, cumin and other spices. Pigs' inner organs were so prized by the Romans that their use was (ineffectually) prohibited by sumptuary laws.

The book of Apicius, our earliest collection of detailed recipes, was actually gathered from many authors from the first century CE onwards. It was written for professional cooks and for prosperous, cosmopolitan people with slaves to do their cooking. Some of the recipes are for the rich, such as those requiring whole animals or expensive spices or wines, but others would have been manageable by middle-class city people. And some are quite simple. Barley soup could be made from a ham knuckle bone. Bacon is simmered with lots of dill, then drizzled with a little oil and salt. Somewhat more elaborate were stews such as *Appian conchicla*, chopped sausage, pork forcemeat, pork shoulder meat and pounded spices combined with cooked dried peas, covered with *liquamen*, wine and oil, and cooked over a gentle fire. (*Liquamen*, the ubiquitous Roman fish sauce, was something like today's Thai fish sauce.) In another stew, *Matian minutal*, beef meatballs and diced cooked shoulder of pork with its crackling were cooked in seasoned *liquamen* and stock, and then combined with diced Matian apples, spices, vinegar, honey and *defrutum* (boiled-down fruit syrup); finally, the sauce was thickened with crumbled *tracta* (dried raw pastry). Pork shoulder could be simmered with barley and figs, coated with honey and browned in a red-hot frying pan to crisp the fat, then served with a sauce of sweet raisin wine and buns made with wine. Pig's stomach could be stuffed with pounded pork, brains, raw eggs and strong flavourings, then boiled or roasted. Its testicles could also be stuffed and roasted, as could the uterus.

Some of Apicius' more luxurious dishes seem to have been devised to show off the chef's ingenuity. Roman chefs often aimed to transform the basic ingredient of a dish, as by covering meat with a sweet sauce that contained eight or ten herbs and spices, as well as wine, honey and *liquamen*. One elaborate casserole was made by lining a deep mould with caul fat, covering this with oil and roasted pine nuts and then cooked dried peas, followed by a layer of boiled pork cubes and chopped roasted sausages; the layers were repeated, ending with peas. Over this was poured a sauce made by cooking belly pork with *liquamen*, water, leek, green coriander, forcemeat, fowl, brains and spices. Then the dish was covered and baked, and finally it was turned out on a dish and decorated with a garnish of hard-boiled egg whites pounded with white pepper, pine nuts, honey, white wine and *liquamen*. There are seventeen recipes for the most luxurious pork dish of all: roast suckling piglet. One calls for stuffing the pig with a mixture of chicken forcemeat, meat from thrushes and figpeckers, sausages, pitted dates, dried bulbs, shelled snails, mallows, beetroot, leeks, celery, boiled cabbage, coriander, peppercorns, pine nuts, fifteen eggs and *liquamen*. After it is roasted, it should be split open along its back and covered with a sauce of pepper, rue, *liquamen*, sweet raisin wine, honey and oil, thickened with starch.

For luxury tables, the Romans kept short-legged pigs in sties, where they might fatten them on grain, or even figs and honeyed wine. They imported their hams from Gaul, however, where the people had been curing hams from 1000 BCE. The Gauls lived in thickly wooded country with lots of oak forests, ideal country for raising tasty pigs, which roamed half-wild and were caught when their meat was required. The Gauls were known for devouring huge quantities of meat, especially fresh and salted pork, at their feasts.

The Romans had several types of sausages, such as Lucanian sausages, made of highly seasoned ground pork, smoked above the fireplace and not otherwise cooked. Sausages have been developed in every country in Europe. They include French andouillettes, filled with chitterlings (the small intestines of pigs that also form their casings); Genoa salami, made of chopped raw pork and fat, highly seasoned with garlic, salt and spices, then air-dried, smoked and aged; Polish *krakowska* (called kielbasa in the US), finely ground pork and fat and beef, seasoned with garlic and herbs, and smoked; Spanish chorizo, pork flavoured with sweet and hot peppers and smoked; Greek *loukanika*, small pieces of pork belly marinated in seasoned red wine and dried or poached; Swedish *julkorv*, Christmas potato sausage, made of equal parts of finely ground beef, pork and potatoes, and poached; and many, many more. Germany has developed about 300 varieties: every little region has its local *Würste*. A few examples are *Leberwurst*, a cooked sausage made of liver homogenized with fat; *Teewurst*, a smooth, highly spiced paste of raw pork, sometimes combined with beef, and cured; and *Blutwurst*, a cooked sausage made of pig's blood, studded with pieces of fat and sometimes bits of tongue. All these are eaten as is. Sausages can be delicacies but have also been a traditional food for poor people, especially when they are loaded with grain filler; British sausages may be up to 50 per cent cereal. The nineteenth-century journalist Henry Mayhew mentions faggots, a poor person's sausage made of equal parts of pork inner organs and fat and of breadcrumbs or oatmeal, seasoned, wrapped in caul and baked.

For many centuries, pigs remained the most important source of meat for Europeans. In early medieval England, the idea of roaming, foraging pigs was so familiar that some woods were measured in the Domesday Book by the number of swine they could support. Large landowners sent their flocks into the forest with a swineherd, like Gurth in Walter Scott's *Ivanhoe*; and every moderately prosperous peasant family kept a pig, which could be maintained at practically no cost. Pigs did not require pastures like cattle or sheep, but could forage on their own, in the woods, by the roadside and even in city streets. Poor city dwellers continued to raise pigs well into the nineteenth century. Friedrich Engels reported that pigs roamed freely through the narrow streets of the

Leberwurst (US: Liverwurst), normally made with pig's liver.

Italian charcuterie: regional salamis and sausages.

Sleeping Swineherd, 1876, engraving.

Manchester slums, 'snuffling among the garbage heaps', and were also kept in sties in nearly every interior court.[3] Into the nineteenth century cities such as Naples actually relied on pigs to clean up their streets. Rural owners, and those who were more particular about the quality of their pork, confined their pigs and fed them on house and garden scraps.

Professional brewers or the many farmers who brewed beer at home could feed pigs cost-free from the mash left after the beer was taken off, as could dairy farmers from the whey left over from making cheese. E. B. White's Wilbur (in *Charlotte's Web*, 1952) shows how recently pigs could be nicely maintained at practically no cost to the farmer. Wilbur's meals include 'skim milk, wheat midlings [by-products of flour-grinding, including bran], leftover pancakes, half a doughnut, the rind of a summer squash, two pieces of stale toast, a third

King Arthur meets a giant who is roasting a pig, *c.* 1325–75, French manuscript illumination.

'Pig Killing', watercolour illustration for the month of December from a medieval calendar.

of a ginger snap, a fish tail, one orange peel, several noodles from a noodle soup, the scum off a cup of cocoa, an ancient jelly-roll, a strip of paper from the lining of the garbage pail, and a spoonful of raspberry jello'.[4]

Pigs were slaughtered in November or December, when the weather was cool. Fresh pork had to be eaten immediately in the days before refrigeration, and the rest was preserved. The pig would be hoisted upside down and killed by a quick knife-cut to the carotid artery, which would render it unconscious by cutting off blood to its brain but let the heart continue pumping, forcing a gush of blood from the wound that could be collected for black puddings. The highly perishable blood would be packed into a stomach or intestines, mixed with spices and offal, fat, cereal and sometimes onions, and cooked. This blood sausage or pudding might be eaten at once or dried to be eaten a few weeks later. Some parts of the meat would be eaten fresh. The sides would be strewn with salt, stacked in a trough with a gutter to drain away the brine that forms, and left for about six weeks. Then they were hung to dry in a cool, airy place, and finally smoked by hanging in the chimney, not too close to the fire, over wood smoke for about a month.

Properly made and stored, according to William Cobbett, the bacon should 'be as good at the end of the year as on the first day'.[5] Generally, a poor family would sell the choicest parts, roasts and hams, and enrich their own meals through the year with bacon and sausage. Samuel Sidney explained in the nineteenth century that 'there is no savings bank for a labourer like a pig' because a piglet could be bought for a sovereign in early summer, fed on household waste and killed at Christmas. Then the farmer could sell the hams 'to buy another pig, and the rest will remain for his own consumption, without seeming to have cost anything'.[6]

Butchering a pig in a 16th-century Dutch etching.

David Teniers the Younger, *Sausage Making*, 1642, oil on canvas.

No wonder the annual pig killing was an occasion for celebration: for poor people, in many parts of Europe and Asia, it typically represented their sole source of meat. Although the poorest peasants got no meat at all, those who were slightly better off got bacon: Piers Plowman had no meat, but the yeoman in William Langland's poem had flitches of bacon. Bacon was often combined with dried legumes, since both could be stored through the winter. The salt pork enlivened the legumes, while their blandness moderated the saltiness of the pork. The classic British version was pork and pease pudding, in which a preparation of seasoned, mashed dried peas was wrapped in a cloth and boiled in the cooking liquid of a piece of cured pork.

In *Cottage Economy* (1823), Cobbett expatiated on the pig's contributions to the welfare of the labouring class. Indeed,

Arnoldo Van Westerhout, *Three Men Castrate a Pig*, 1765, etching.

he claimed, the sight of 'a couple of flitches of bacon' in his house did more 'to keep a man from poaching and stealing' than 'fifty thousand Methodist sermons and religious tracts' or 'whole volumes of penal statutes'. If labourers are poor and underfed, it is partly because they disdain products of the pig – bacon and lard – that could keep them healthy and happy. Cobbett recommended that a cottager buy a pig at four months old, when it could support itself on what it could pick up in the fields or by the road, supplemented by kitchen and garden waste – at virtually no cost to its owner. When it approached a year old, it should be fattened on grain. A cottager's family could subsist nicely for a week on the products of a pig immediately after slaughter: organs and hog's puddings made from the blood. 'The butcher, the next day, cuts the hog up, and then the house is filled with meat! Souse, griskins, blade-bones, thigh-bones, spare-ribs, chines, belly-pieces, cheeks, all coming into use one after the other, and the last of the latter not before the end of about four or five weeks.' What remains, the two sides or flitches, is cured for bacon, which will provide the family with meat until the following Christmas. Bacon 'is always ready; as good cold as hot; goes to the field or the coppice conveniently . . . has twice as much strength in it as any other thing of the same weight'. Lard was equally important. Country children ought

The Pig Pye Man, c. 1820, engraving.

to be happy with sweet lard spread upon bread; they were badly brought up if they insisted on butter.[7] Lard was very important in northern Europe, where vegetable oils would have to be imported and butter was reserved for the prosperous; lard (and bacon) provided the necessary fat in poor

The German delicacy of *schmalz* (lard) on bread.

people's diets, as well as flavour in dishes made of cheap, bland ingredients.

More prosperous people ate a good deal of meat, which doctors told them was the best food for maintaining health. The middle classes expected at least one large piece of meat for dinner (except on the large number of meatless fast days in Catholic countries); the rich expected a wide selection of meat, poultry and seafood. The fourteenth-century *The Good Wife's Guide* (*Le Ménagier de Paris*, written by a wealthy Parisian bourgeois to instruct his young wife on her duties, including cooking and meal planning), gives a good idea of high-end middle-class menus. His dinner menus always focus on a roast, and he gives recipes for spit-roasted pork, served with spring onions (scallions) and verjuice (the sour juice of unripe grapes or other fruit); an elaborately stuffed roast piglet; boiled salt ham; and fresh ham cooked in saffroned stock and grain verjuice, with ginger and bread, served with mashed grape sauce. Pork, usually preserved, often appears as a side dish in his menus – sausages, roasted boar's tail, salted pork chine, aspic of pig – and it is used to flavour or enhance dishes such as pea soup and rabbit stew; lard adds a last touch to fresh peas, as we would use butter. When a minor prince went on crusade in 1345 and left directions for his wife's management of the household, he stipulated that it was to be limited to 30 persons and that they were to be allotted one freshly killed pig per week and 30 salted pigs per year.

Beef was neither common nor desirable at this time, because cattle were generally kept for dairy or labour and were killed only when old and tough. Veal was desirable, but it could not be easily preserved. Pork, on the other hand, could be even better when preserved. Still, because pigs were common and cured pork was what poor people had to eat, pork seldom appears as the central attraction in royal menus or in high-end cookbooks. Fowl, domestic and wild, and game were preferred for grand banquets. (Chicken, although now such a thrifty option, was relatively expensive until well into the nineteenth century, and game was valued because hunting was restricted to the upper class.)

Only roast suckling pig was still a luxurious food. These piglets, which have been fed only on mother's milk, may be killed from two to six weeks old, but are best at three to four weeks. Suckling pigs were still generally available in the nineteenth century, although they are now rarely seen. (Nevertheless, there are recipes for it in Julia Child's *Mastering the Art of French Cooking* (1970) – and even in Irma Rombauer's *The Joy of Cooking* (2006 edition).) Wild boar remained an aristocratic meat because it had to be obtained by hunting, an upper-class prerogative. The head was an especially festive dish. Alexis Soyer, the eminent Victorian chef, describes the elaborate way it was prepared. After scraping off the hair and boning the head without scratching the skin, you soak it for eight to ten days in salt with brown sugar and spices. Then you stuff it with pork forcemeat, bacon, truffles and pistachios, and sew it up to recreate the shape of the head. Then you simmer it in a rich, seasoned stock for seven to eight hours. After it has cooled, you glaze it and supply it with eyes (balls of lard studded with truffles) and tusks (baked dough) and decorate it with fresh flowers. As wild boars became hard to find, pigs' heads might be treated in the same way. The writer of the *Ménagier de Paris*, eager to imitate the aristocracy, gave his wife directions for making pork taste like wild boar.

Although seldom appearing as the main dish at an aristocratic dinner, pork was widely used in medieval cookery. Banquets and even formal dinners up through the nineteenth century consisted of three main courses, each made up of eight or ten dishes – like successive buffets – and typically each would include a pork side dish such as pies filled with minced pork, dried fruits, spices and eggs or, more extravagantly, meatballs of ground pork, sausage meat, spices, egg and currants, baked, painted gold with saffron, covered with honey and garnished with slices of fried apples sprinkled with cinnamon. Inner organs were served at high-class meals, because liver, kidneys, testes, sweetbreads, brains and bone marrow were still considered delicacies. When the sensualist Sir Epicure Mammon (in Ben Jonson's *Alchemist* 2:1) imagines a fabulously luxurious banquet, he adds to his list of exotic meats

the swelling unctuous paps
Of a fat pregnant sow, newly cut off,
Drest with an exquisite, and poignant sauce.

Brawn, made of the gelatinous, fatty meat of the head, was a highly popular first-course side dish, traditionally served at Christmas. At first it was made from wild boar, but after they became rare by the sixteenth century, it was made from pig. The head was lightly cured in brine, then boiled and boned. Because this meat is gelatinous, its cooking broth is rich enough to be boiled down to make a jelly. In medieval times the head was kept in a pot in a pickling liquid of ale, salt and verjuice. The flesh could be served with vinegar and pepper, or in a thick spiced syrup of wine with honey or sugar, or with ground almonds and sugar. From the eighteenth century on the chopped brawn was set in a moulded jelly formed by its rich cooking liquid. Now it is usually moulded in a cylindrical shape like a cheese – hence its American name 'head cheese'.

Pieds de Porc à la Sainte Menehould, an elaborate preparation of pigs' trotters, is said to date back to the time of Charles VII in the fifteenth century. Alexandre Dumas tells how the king was stranded in the country and required a meal from the local peasants. At their wits' end to produce a suitable dish, they simmered pigs' trotters with vegetables, herbs and wine for an hour and a half, then stripped the meat from the bones and dipped it in milk and egg, then breadcrumbs; finally they broiled (grilled) the meat, basting it with melted butter. The king found the dish delicious. (There are several less colourful tales of origin for this dish, but it remains famous and is a boasted local speciality.)

Taillevent's *Le Viandier*, the earliest medieval cookbook, reflects aristocratic tastes: although it includes roast pork recipes, it has more for birds, domestic and wild, and about

Sausage made from head cheese, also known as brawn.

as many for wild boar as for pig. The probable author, Guillaume Tirel, cooked for various members of the French royal family in the later fourteenth century. He suggested that roast pork be served with a sauce made by putting garlic, onions, wine and verjuice in the pan with the drippings from the roast; or else in a pasty with saffron and spice powder, eaten with verjuice. Cold pork could be served in a vinegar and rue sauce, hot boiled fresh pork with a good green sauce of parsley and other herbs, boiled salt pork with mustard. Most of his potages (thick soups or stews) were flavoured by frying the ingredients in bacon grease. He used pigs' trotters and livers to create *entremets*, fanciful dishes served between roast and dessert that aimed to amuse the guests by showing off the chef's ingenuity.

By the seventeenth century beef, veal and mutton were the typical meats on fashionable tables, with pork appearing only in the form of suckling pig or ham, although lard continued to be much used and ground pork was a common ingredient in stuffing. François Pierre de la Varenne cooked for a powerful seventeenth-century French nobleman and is considered the founder of classical French cooking. His *Cuisinier François* (1651) went through 30 editions in 75 years, and his influence reached to most of the aristocratic kitchens of Europe. His usual source of grease was lard or bacon fat, although butter was beginning to come in. He gave recipes for entrées, for the main or second course that followed, and for *entremets*. The entrées for meat days consisted of boiled or fried meat with a sauce; the second course featured a large roasted joint or roasted whole small birds or mammals. La Varenne's entrées include several types of sausages, sautéed and simmered pork tongue, and piglet ragout, which could

Daniel Hopfer, *The Sausage Seller*, 16th century, engraving.

be served cold in the jelly formed by its cooking liquid. His 61 meats that can be served in the second course include comparatively few pork or beef dishes: domestic and wild birds predominate, followed by rabbit and hare, mutton and lamb, and venison. Young wild boar and suckling pig appear on the list, and he provides recipes for a 'Loin of Pork with Sauce Robert' similar to the earlier medieval roast pork recipes. La Varenne's *entremets* include boiled pigs' feet and ears; cold ham pie; sliced ham sautéed in wine or steeped in bouillon and vinegar, covered with breadcrumbs and roasted; and pork tongue sliced and simmered in bouillon, sautéed in lard with vinegar and served with lemon juice, capers and grapes. He gives directions for making Mayence hams – salted and spiced, soaked in lees of wine, buried in the cellar and then hung in the chimney and scented with juniper. Mayence

Piercy Roberts, *Sailors Eating Pork*, 1807, hand-coloured etching. The sailors are protesting that the pork the hostess has served them is still covered with bristles.

George Cruikshank, *A Visit to the Irish Pig! With Reflections Physical and Moral*, 1799, hand-coloured etching. After the Irish rebellion of 1798 was put down, the ex-rebels sent the Enniscorthy boar, a huge, well-formed pig, as a peace offering to George III. The pig was placed in the menagerie at the Tower of London. When the King inspected it, someone joked that the boar had become fat by eating rebels.

ham could be used to make a Basque Pasty: rye piecrust lined with lard and parsley, filled with highly seasoned ham and covered with thick pastry, then baked in a slow oven for fourteen to 30 hours, until the meat is on the point of disintegrating. La Varenne rarely uses pork for the major item in his dinners, and he prefers it in its cured versions.

By the sixteenth century beef was taking its place as the most prized meat in England. Sir Roger North's elaborate dinner for Queen Elizabeth when she visited him in 1578 included nine meat or fish dishes, but pork appeared only in the form of bacon flavouring a dish of oysters and pullets. Accounts for the regular dinners of the Lords of the Star Chamber, running from 1519 to 1639, show them eating mostly beef. They also ate domestic and wild birds and rabbits, but they evidently found pork too plebeian. It appears only once, in the form of brawn, eaten as an appetizer. Henry Fielding's song 'The Roast Beef of Old England' and William Hogarth's painting *Calais Gate* indicate that by the mid-eighteenth century roast beef had come to be considered the quintessentially manly British meat. A nineteenth-century writer even projected this notion back into the Middle Ages, claiming that 'The bowmen who won Cressy and Agincourt were beef-fed.'[8] (Actually, of course, they had to win on bacon.) English people in the early 1980s still looked forward to a joint for Sunday lunch, and they favoured roast beef with Yorkshire pudding.

However, pork remained very popular with the middle classes in the eighteenth century. Hannah Glasse's *The Art of Cookery Made Plain and Easy* (1747), arguably the most successful cookery book of the period, was written for women managing their households with a few servants who had to be trained. Glasse included a large range of pork dishes – roast loin with onions or stuffed with seasoned breadcrumbs and lard and served with spiced apple sauce; hog's feet and ears stewed and then fried; baked pork chops covered with seasoned ground meat and bacon and served with mushroom gravy; fried sausages with apples or pease pudding; a pie filled with leftover cold boiled ham, chicken, hard-boiled egg yolks and rich beef gravy, or one filled with seasoned pork loin strips, apples, sugar and white wine; ham slowly braised with bacon, beef slices, vegetables and herbs and served with an elaborate gravy. Evidently much processing was still done in the home: she tells how to cut a whole pig into parts, make sausages and cure and smoke ham and bacon. The prosperous parson James Woodforde served fish, boiled ham and chicken, roast duck and roast neck of pork at a small dinner party in 1770. Typically, his company dinners consisted of two courses, one of which included pork, ham or bacon.

E. Smith makes much less use of pork in her *Compleat Housewife: or, Accomplish'd Gentlewoman's Companion* (1753), perhaps because she was aiming at a higher-end audience; she was an experienced cook in upper-class British families. She suggests menus for use throughout the year – two menus for each month, with two courses per dinner and usually seven or eight dishes per course. Pork does not appear very frequently (eighteen out of over 350 dishes), and generally in salt form and as a side dish, such as collar of brawn (head cheese) or ham pie, or as a flavouring ingredient for pigeons or chicken. Only once is pork the main item in the main course: roast pig in July. However, her book includes elaborate recipes for ragout of pigs' ears and fricasseed pig.

Alexis Soyer, a Frenchman who became the leading chef in Victorian England, cooked for the upper classes at the Reform Club but also took an interest in food for the working class, including Irish peasants suffering from the famine and British soldiers in the Crimean War. He published highly successful cookbooks appropriate to diverse levels of society. His *Gastronomic Regenerator: A Simplified and Entirely New System of Cookery* (1846) is aimed at the upper or upper middle class and accordingly does not feature pork. 'Pork is a great favourite with some persons,' he writes, 'but scarce ever used for removes, except plain roasted stuffed with sage and onions.' (The remove was the roast or boiled joint that was the main dish of the dinner.) Nevertheless, he proceeds to 'give six new ways of dressing pork for removes', emphasizing that it must be in season (from October to March).[9] They include fresh ham with sauce Robert (a gravy flavoured with vinegar, mustard, gherkin pickles and pickled mushrooms) or breaded with a brown sauce flavoured with ketchup and vinegar, neck

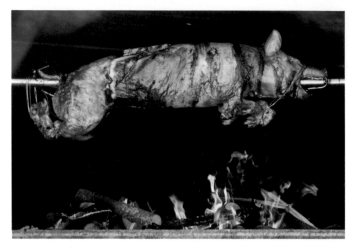

Piglet roasted on a spit.

with remoulade or brown sauce, and spit-roasted stuffed suckling pig. His recipes for side dishes and entrées, smaller meat dishes, also make far less use of pork than of other meats and poultry.

Writing for a middle-class audience in *The Modern Housewife* or *Ménagère* (1851), Soyer was more concerned with economy and spoke better of the pig. 'No animal is more useful for nourishment, and none more indispensable in the kitchen; employed either fresh or salt, all is useful . . . it is the superfluous riches of the farmer, and helps to pay the rent of the cottager.' Nevertheless, there are thirteen recipes for pork among the removes, as compared to 30 for beef and veal and 25 for mutton and lamb. They include spit-roasted leg, chine, spare rib and suckling pig; roast loin or neck with onion-mustard gravy or baked with potatoes, onions and apples; and budget cuts such as boiled bacon with broad beans and boiled pickled pork belly with greens. Ham, curiously, was more fashionable than fresh pork. Ham, Soyer said,

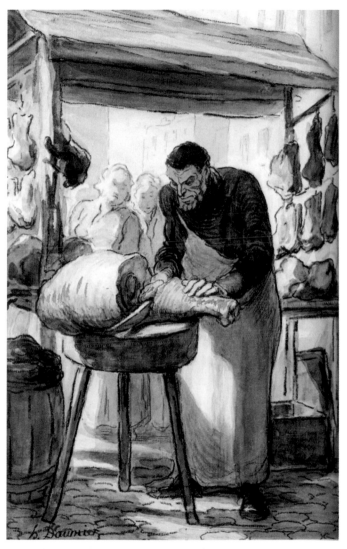

Honoré Daumier, *Pork Butcher in Market Stall*, *c.* 1860, pen and ink and watercolour.

was a 'useful and popular dish . . . equally a favourite in the palace and the cottage, may be dressed in upwards of fifty different ways, with as many different dishes'. It may be served hot, glazed or covered with breadcrumbs. Pork entrées, besides the cutlets that he also suggested for aristocratic dinners, included kidneys and dishes made from leftovers, such as a tasty pork hash and fried ham slices served with a purée of creamed peas. Bacon or ham form the base for a number of vegetable soups, including a 'very economical' French cabbage soup, made by boiling two pounds of streaky pickled pork or bacon with two pounds of cabbage, a few root vegetables, and a bunch of celery.[10] The experienced housewife who speaks for Soyer in this book ends with representative bills of fare for her family's dinners when they were just starting out, when business became better, and now that they are prosperous. They had pork for their main dish twice in the first sample week, but it appears only rarely, as a side dish, in their days of greater prosperity. As a climax, she reproduces the menu of an elaborate dinner given at the Reform Club, at which the only pork dish was *Jambon en surprise glacé à la Vanille*, evidently one of the sweets.

Soyer's *A Shilling Cookery Book for the People* (1854), written for the prosperous working-class cook, gave more emphasis to pork, but not as much as might be expected. Chiefly, he recommended cheaper cuts and a lesser proportion of meat to vegetables. *Soyer's Standard Cookery for the People* (1859), aimed at a slightly lower class – 'the artisan, mechanic, and cottager' – makes considerable use of pork but puts principal emphasis on making a little meat go a long way, as in bacon in split pea soup, ham in carrot soup, peas panada (bacon flavouring a purée of split peas), Indian Meal Poullenta (pork, sausage or beef slices placed between two layers of cooked cornmeal mush, baked briefly and served with gravy or treacle), and

William Claesz. Heda, *Laid Table with Ham and Roll*, 1635, oil on wood.

Carthusian of Meat and Vegetables (pigs' tongues, feet, bacon, ham, liver, sausages or other types of meat covered with a lot of cabbage and baked for two hours); the idea was that Carthusians, forbidden to eat meat, hid it under layers of permitted food.

Isabella Beeton compiled her *Book of Household Management* (1861) from recipes she requested and got from housewives all over Britain, so it is probably an accurate reflection of what the British middle classes were eating at the time. Although she disdains the pig for its gluttony, laziness and indiscriminate eating habits, she admits that 'there is no domestic animal so profitable or so useful to man as the much-maligned pig, or any that yields him a more varied or more luxurious repast'. Moreover, 'his fat . . . is quite as important as his flesh, and brings a price equal to the best joints in the carcase',[11] for lard was still essential for frying and baking. She provides 25 pork recipes, about as many as for mutton and lamb but considerably less than for beef and veal. Some of her pork recipes were high-end – roast pork loin, roast fresh ham, cured ham covered with breadcrumbs or glaze, roast suckling pig artfully arranged on its platter. Her roast pork is done in the characteristically British style, with the rind intact so as to produce a crisp coat of crackling. The rind is scored before roasting so that it does not shrink and deform the meat, and for serving it is lifted away and cut into thin, crisp strips to be placed around the meat. In France and the US the rind is removed and the roast is basted to produce a rich glaze on the fat. Beeton, like cooks of many nations, recommends that the pork be served with apple sauce.

She also offers budget recipes – bacon fried, broiled or boiled and served with vegetables; dishes made of leftover pork loin heated in sauce or ground in a pork loaf; a casserole of sliced liver and lights (lungs), parboiled potatoes, bacon, seasonings and onions baked for two hours ('a savoury and economical dish'); pigs' feet simmered with liver, heart and bacon in seasoned gravy. She uses ham and bacon extensively to flavour stock and soups, poultry and rabbit dishes, and vegetables; and she explains how to lard lean meat. (Larding, threading strips of lard into a piece of meat, is a technique that goes back to the Middle Ages, when it was particularly important to mitigate the dryness of game. It is still used but, as Julia Child says, more to give a showy appearance than to improve the meat.)

Beeton adds an extensive list of suggested menus, for both formal entertaining and family meals. Dinner parties were an important Victorian status symbol: middle-class families aimed to give a dinner party once a month; the upper classes, once a week. And the middle class had to make use of their leftovers. Pork is never the star attraction in Beeton's elaborate bills of fare, but it appears regularly. It almost has to, because

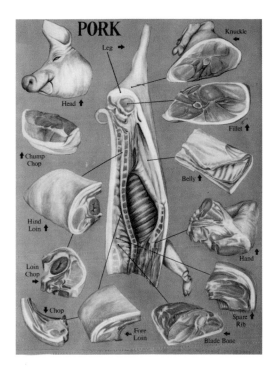

Cuts of pork from Mrs Beeton's *All About Cookery* (1962 edn).

PORK

Knuckle

Leg →

Head ↑

Fillet ↑

↑ Chump Chop

Belly ↑

Hind Loin ↑

Hand ↑

Loin Chop →

↓ Chop

Spare Rib ↑

← Fore Loin

Blade Bone ←

her fanciest dinners for eighteen people include four courses with a total of over twenty dishes. So pork makes its appearance in side dishes such as veal and ham pie and broiled ham garnished with cauliflowers. 'Plain family dinners', which generally include two courses with main dishes plus dessert, use pork more prominently. Beeton suggests menus for a week's dinners throughout the year. Pork cutlets with tomato sauce might be served on Tuesday, boiled leg of pork with greens, potatoes and pease pudding on Thursday, pea soup made from the liquid the pork was boiled in and cold pork on Friday. Roast suckling pig with tomato sauce and brain sauce might be the star of Sunday dinner, with its leftovers served on Monday; bacon and greens were suggested for

A traditional pork pie with English mustard.

Friday. For another week, pork cutlets with tomato sauce are again suggested for Tuesday and roast leg of pork for three days – freshly roasted on Thursday, then served cold on Friday and curried on Saturday.

Catherine (Mrs Charles) Dickens's published collection of her bills of fare (1852), consisting of 72 dinners for two to three persons, 39 for four to five, 32 for six to seven, 25 for eight to ten, and five for fourteen to twenty, gives a good idea of what a prosperous upper-middle-class family, fond of entertaining, might serve in the mid-nineteenth century. Her relatively simple meals for two to three people consisted of soup or fish, two meat dishes accompanied by vegetables and potatoes, and one or two desserts. Fresh or cured pork appears in many menus, although less often than mutton, fowl or beef. In twelve of the 72 menus, one of the two meat dishes is pork: cutlets, bacon, pickled pork, calves' liver and bacon, boiled knuckles of ham, and minced beef or mutton with bacon. The 71 more elaborate bills of fare for four to seven persons usually include a roast of mutton, fowl or beef. Roast pork, evidently suckling pig, appears in one unusually luxurious dinner, which also includes roast beef, fancy seafood dishes and three meat entrées; but in no other does pork take a central position. However, Dickens did often serve pork side dishes, especially in her dinners for eight to twenty people, in order to make up her total of up to 28 dishes. These could be any of the main meats served at family dinners, as well as macaroni and bacon, minced mutton with bacon, cold ham, veal and ham patties, pig's jaw with beans, or Brunswick sausage. On a visit to France, she discovered pigs' feet stuffed with truffles at a Parisian restaurant, and in 1854 she added this dish to her menus. She was very particular about the quality of her hams. Once she ordered a ham from London when the family was on vacation, which appeared as a boiled knuckle of ham for the first night's dinner, was served cold in thin slices at the next meal, and finally was mixed with veal as a filling for patty shells.

In the past, large pieces of bacon were boiled and served hot or cold with mustard as the main meat. In present-day Britain, bacon is most often fried in thin slices and served for breakfast. Bacon or sausage are standard items in a full British breakfast. As in past centuries, smoked pork is seen far more than fresh. While roast pork with crackling and apple sauce remains a classic British dish, roast beef and even roast lamb are more frequently served. A modern gourmet pub in Lancashire serves pigs' trotters in a puddle of rich sauce, boned and filled with diced meat in a contrasting sauce.

The French, too, are less apt to feature pork than other meats as the centrepiece of a formal dinner; fresh pork is not prominent in haute cuisine. Auguste Escoffier, in *The Complete Guide to the Art of Modern Cookery* (1903), decreed that 'Large joints of fresh pork are used more frequently in household or Bourgeois cookery than in the professional kitchen.' In fact, 'without the culinary value of its hams', pork would hold little place in the classical kitchen. Only 'the ham provides a valuable resource . . . whether it be Bayonne, York, Prague or Westphalian'.[12] He gives 306 beef recipes to 106 for pork and ham.

Nevertheless, in *Mastering the Art of French Cooking* (1970), Child, Bertholle and Beck include several recipes for roast pork and chops, a recipe for roast suckling pig only slightly less elaborate than the medieval versions, and creative variations for serving cooked ham, such as *Jambon Braisé Morvandelle*: sauté carrots and onions in a casserole, cover with slices of ham, add herbs, spices, white wine and stock, and simmer in a slow oven for two hours; dust with powdered sugar and glaze in a hot oven; then boil down the braising liquid, add mushrooms, shallots, Madeira and cream, and simmer for five minutes. French cuisine makes the most of pork as an enhancement to other dishes – salt pork, ham or bacon may be used as a flavouring for cabbage vegetable soup, tomato sauce, quiches and gratins, casserole-roasted chicken, beef

Advertisement for White's 'Victoria' brand breakfast bacon and hams, 1899.

stews, red cabbage and sauerkraut; and ground ham or pork as an ingredient in stuffings for roulade of beef or boned shoulder of lamb or roast veal.

Long ago the French, like many other peoples, discovered what a bit of pork can do for a meal of beans. *La Potée*

Camille Pissarro, *The Pork Butcher*, 1883, oil on canvas.

Alsacienne is a budget dish, using only one pound of lean salt pork or smoked butt with many vegetables – two cups of dried white beans, two onions, a cabbage, a cauliflower, two cups each of peas and green beans, a head of celery, three carrots and three potatoes. *Cassoulet* is a vastly more elaborate version of pork and beans. In Child's version, white beans are simmered with fresh bacon, onions, boiled pork rind and herbs; chunks of boned mutton shoulder, cracked mutton bones, and onions are browned in pork fat; the mutton and bones are simmered with garlic, tomatoes, herbs, white wine and stock for an hour and a half, and the bones are discarded; the beans are added and simmered for five minutes, and a layer of this mixture is placed in a casserole. This is covered with layers of mutton chunks, of bacon and roast pork loin chunks, and of browned sausage patties, ending with beans and sausage patties. Cooking juices from the meats and beans are poured over the casserole, breadcrumbs and parsley are spread over it and pork roasting fat is dribbled on top. The whole is baked in a moderate oven for an hour, during which the crust is broken up periodically and mixed into the casserole. Jane Grigson's version is even more elaborate: two types of sausage are added to the beans; and a layer of pork and goose ragout, cut-up pork shoulder and preserved goose simmered with onions, tomatoes, stock and seasoning, is placed in the casserole.

Fresh pork fat is essential in all pâtés to keep the meats from becoming dry or heavy, and the classic *Terrine de Foie de Porc*, a glorified liverwurst, is made by lining a pâté dish with sheets of pork fat, filling it with pork fat ground together with liver and puréed rice mixed with egg and seasonings, covering it with pork fat and foil, and baking it in a pan of

Cassoulet made with goose meat, pork sausage and beans.

water for an hour and a half. The French have an enormous variety of charcuterie, in which pork is the main or an essential ingredient – sausages, hams, pâtés and terrines.

Germany has an even richer array of sausages. And dinner is very likely to centre on a large piece of pork. *Kasseler Rippenspeer*, rib roast served on sauerkraut with mashed potatoes and a rich wine and sour cream gravy; *Eisbein*, braised pig knuckles often served with pease pudding and potatoes; and *Schweinepfeffer*, a highly seasoned pork ragout thickened with pig's blood, are just a few examples. The pork and sauerkraut combination extends over central Europe: roast pork with dumplings and sauerkraut is a classic Czech dish, and Hungary's *Szekely Goulash* consists of pork shoulder and kielbasa cooked for a long time with sauerkraut, green pepper, paprika and

Pâté de campagne.

Dried meats produced at a smokehouse in Croatia.

other seasonings, with sour cream added at the end. Slovakia's national dish is gnocchi-like dumplings topped with soft sheep's cheese and bits of bacon fat. The Slovaks stuff potato pancakes with *Diabolske soté*, devil's sauté, a mixture of pork and hot peppers.

Pork meatballs and roast pork with crackling are classic Danish dishes. In southern Europe, Italians cook cabbage with salt pork and sausages and simmer white beans with hard sausages and parsley sautéed in pork fat. *Cocido*, the national stew of Spain, is made of many salted parts of a pig (head, shoulder hams, backbone, tail, ribs, snout, ears, trotters, streaky bacon), chorizo and lard, as well as beef tongue, veal, a hen, chickpeas, broad beans, potatoes and greens – all simmered for hours. The fact that Jews and Moors could not eat pork seems to have heightened its appeal to Spanish Christians.

Germany, Denmark, Poland and Austria consume the most pork per person per year of all countries. According to the US Department of Agriculture data for 2006, 43.9 kilograms of pork are consumed per capita annually in the European Union, 40 in the People's Republic of China, and 29 in the US.

4
Pork in the New World

Early Spanish explorers brought pigs to the Americas, and they learned from the Caribbean peoples a fine new method for cooking them: barbecue (probably derived from Taino *barabicu*) – cooking in the smoke of an open fire. Barbecuing is the slow-cooking of meat over coals, using smoke more than fire; the fire must be just hot enough to cook the meat without drying it out. This technique works especially well for the succulent meat of pigs. The traditional barbecue, as still practised in rural areas in the south-eastern US, involves placing a rack over a hole in the ground or a wide, shallow container and placing a whole, split dressed hog on the rack. A constant supply of hardwood logs burned down to coals is shovelled under the meat, which cooks anywhere from eight to fifteen hours, without added sauce or basting. When the meat is ready to fall off the bone, it is pulled into shreds. In urban areas, separate cuts such as shoulder and rib are more common. Barbecue can be simulated at home by baking a boneless pork loin in a very hot oven for fifteen minutes, then in a very slow oven for five hours, then smoking it over soaked wood chips on a grill for ten minutes. Pork is the meat for barbecue in North Carolina, Mississippi, Alabama and Tennessee; in Oklahoma, Missouri, Kansas and Texas it is beef. Traditionally the cooked meat was splashed with a thin, sharp sauce of vinegar and red pepper, but often the sauce is ketchup-based. Barbecue may be topped with coleslaw and served in a bun.

All the European settlers naturally brought pigs with them, as well as recipes that they often modified to use New World ingredients. Scrapple is a Pennsylvania Dutch adaptation of a traditional German meal pudding prepared from scraps at butchering time, bound together with cereal; scrapple uses cornmeal, an American cereal. Pork scraps are simmered until they fall apart, and cornmeal is dribbled in to thicken the mixture to the consistency of mush, while it is seasoned with salt, pepper and sage. Then it is poured into loaf pans and cooled. At serving time, it is cut into slices and lightly fried.

At first American pigs ran free, foraging in the local woods, and thus could be maintained for practically nothing. They ran 'hog wild' and multiplied rapidly. As Robert Beverley remarked in 1705, 'the Hogs run where they list, and find their own support in the Woods, without any Care of the Owner.'[1] Because of frontier conditions, pigs could be let to run unconfined much later in the American countryside than in most parts of Europe. Besides, legal restrictions were looser. Pigs roamed the streets of New York, Boston and Philadelphia well into the nineteenth century. When New York finally banned pigs from the streets, housewives protested.

Of course, many farmers did confine their pigs, and could feed them as European farmers did, with waste such as whey from the dairy, cabbage leaves, turnip tops and windfall apples. Moreover, it soon became apparent that corn (*Zea mays*), a major American crop, was excellent for fattening pigs. Corn and soybeans are the basic elements in commercial pig feed today. In fact, hogs eat about half of the huge annual corn crop of the US. In addition, pork was relatively easy to preserve and could be stored without refrigeration; ham and bacon could last a year, and pork pieces could be kept from six months to a year in a barrel of brine solution.

Increasingly, pigs were raised in confinement and fed a prepared feed, and American pig production became centred in the Corn Belt of the Midwest. Cincinnati, Ohio, became famous for 'packing fifteen bushels of corn into a hog, packing the hog into a barrel, and packing a barrel into a train or a flat boat'.[2] Later, when railroads became the main carriers of freight, pig processing was centred in Chicago. With the spread of iceboxes and then refrigerators and the development of refrigerated railroad cars, it became possible for many people to enjoy fresh pork all year round. Today most of America's pigs live in Iowa and other Midwestern states, although an

A prize hog on a Midwestern farm, 1923.

James Dean visiting his uncle's farm in Indiana, February 1955.

ingenious entrepreneur also developed concentrated industrial pig farming in the otherwise unproductive countryside
of eastern North Carolina.

Laura Ingalls Wilder describes pig-keeping in a prosperous farm family on the Wisconsin frontier. At first their pig
'ran wild in the Big Woods, living on acorns and nuts and
roots'. As winter came, Pa 'caught it and put it in a pen made
of logs, to fatten. He would butcher it as soon as the weather
was cold enough to keep the pork frozen.' Pa killed the pig
with the assistance of Uncle Henry, first boiling a great kettle
of water. Little Laura did not like to hear the pig squeal –
although her father assured her the stabbing did not hurt him
because it was so quick – but 'After that, Butchering Time
was great fun . . . there would be spare-ribs for dinner, and
Pa had promised Laura and Mary the bladder and the pig's
tail.' Once the hog was dead, Pa and Uncle Henry scalded the
body in the boiling water, scraped off its bristles with their
knives, gutted it and hung it up to cool. Then they cut it up
into 'hams and shoulders, side meat and spare-ribs and belly
. . . the heart and the liver and the tongue, and the head . . .
and the dish-pan full of bits to be made into sausage'. Every
piece was sprinkled with salt, and the hams and shoulders
were set to pickle in brine, to be smoked later. Pa blew up the
bladder and gave it to the girls to play with; then, as a special
treat, they roasted and ate the tail. Ma spent the next two days
trying out the lard, skimming out the cracklings (in the US, the
crisp residue left after fat has been melted) as they formed to
be used later to flavour Johnny-cake. She made head cheese by
boiling the head until the meat fell off the bones, chopping
the meat fine, seasoning it with salt and spices, and mixing in
the pot-liquor; then she put it in a pan to cool and set, and
served it cut in slices. She chopped the odd bits of meat and
fat, seasoned them with salt, pepper and sage, mixed them

71

well, and moulded the mixture into balls, which she set out in the shed to freeze so they would be good to eat all winter. 'When Butchering Time was over, there were the sausages and the headcheese, the big jars of lard and the keg of white salt pork out in the shed, and in the attic hung the smoked hams and shoulders.'[3]

Of course this family that could eat the hams from their pigs was a prosperous one. Others had to sell their fresh pork and hams. The most common form of preserved pork was not bacon, as in England, but the more easily prepared barrel pork: that is, large pieces of pork kept submerged in a barrel of brine. This was the standard meat for poor to middle-class people and for the army from the Revolutionary through to the Civil War. In the War of 1812 so much pork was supplied to American soldiers by a New York packer called 'Uncle Sam' Wilson that he came to personify the entire government and was portrayed by cartoonists as a giant figure in a tall hat under a banner that read 'Uncle Sam is feeding the Army'. Barrelled pork was graded according to the pig parts included, from barrels containing only the sides of large hogs to barrels that could contain any part, including the head and feet. Well-to-do working-class families got the better varieties, slaves the lowest grade. The former prominence of barrel pork survives in the idioms of 'scraping the bottom of the barrel' and 'pork barrel legislation'. The latter refers to laws that take money from general taxation revenues to fund projects that benefit only a particular legislator's constituents; the derivation seems to be that a public resource is being directed to serve a private interest.

The taste must have been inferior to that of well-prepared bacon – Cobbett insisted that pork must be well drained in curing, for leaving it sopping in brine gave 'it the sort of taste that barrel pork and sea junk have, than which there is nothing

Poster advertising Fowler Brothers Ltd, pork packers and lard refiners, late 19th century.

more villainous'.[4] But many Americans relished barrel pork. A frontier housewife in James Fenimore Cooper's *The Chainbearer* (1845) thinks of it as the mark of a decent standard of living. She takes for granted that people will have bread and potatoes, 'but I hold a family to be in a desperate way when the mother can see the bottom of the pork barrel. Give me the children that's raised on good sound pork afore all the game in the country . . . pork is the staff of life.'[5] Strangers were not so enthusiastic. A Norwegian immigrant to Iowa recorded in her diary in 1854: 'The dishes here vary from boiled pork to fried pork, rare to well done', along with coffee, bread and butter, pickles, and now and then potatoes and fried onions. 'This is our meal, morning, noon and evening . . . Oh that I had some new potatoes and mackerel from home!'[6] Starting on a journey from Kentucky to Texas in the 1850s, Frederick Law Olmsted cheerfully ate salt pork and corn bread, because he did not realize that for the next six months he should see 'nothing else'.[7]

Prosperous people, of course, enjoyed fresh pork and hams, along with other meats, especially after refrigeration became available toward the middle of the nineteenth century. However, the traditional diet did not change much in isolated southern and western communities. As Henry Adams wrote, 'Indian corn was the national crop, and Indian corn was eaten three times a day in another form as salt pork.'[8] In one community in the Blue Ridge Mountains in 1929, even in late summer when food was most plentiful, the regular diet consisted of fried fat back, corn pone and thickened gravy for breakfast; oatmeal, pone, biscuit, preserves and coffee for dinner; and fat back, pone, milk (occasionally) and coffee for supper.

In general among all classes, Americans got more meat than their counterparts in Europe, and pork was their favourite, as well as most widely consumed, meat until well into the twentieth century. Frederick Marryat marvelled at the plentitude of pork available in the US. Visiting New York on 4 July in the 1830s, he described Broadway, three miles long,

American-style crispy fried bacon.

as lined with booths selling roast pork. And the same was true in every other city or village in the US.

Pork became increasingly convenient to cook – from a country ham that required soaking, long simmering and laborious removal of the rind to a precooked ham that needed only to be placed in the oven and heated; from a greasy four- to ten-pound slab of bacon to a neat package of slices, first marketed in 1915. Lard has been superseded by Crisco, a vegetable-oil-based shortening introduced in 1911. Proctor & Gamble managed to persuade American housewives that the tastelessness of Crisco is actually an advantage: girls prefer that 'the fat which supplies their growing bodies with energy should be in the purest and most inviting form and should be one that their digestions welcome, rather than repel'.[9] But something has been lost. Bacon and ham are not as tasty as they used to be. Compare a 1904 recipe for country ham soaked, simmered with vinegar and spices, spread with vinegar, mustard, breadcrumbs, sugar, cloves, raisins and sherry, and baked, with a 1939 recipe for precooked ham covered with canned pineapple, maraschino cherries and lots of brown sugar, and heated in the oven. In general, Americans tend to make their pork too sweet. An extreme example is Indiana Pork Cake, composed of ground fresh fat pork, raisins, dates, citron, flour, spices and lots of molasses and brown sugar.

Perhaps the most extreme example of convenience pork is Spam. It is a neat rectangle of cooked, cured pork and fat that can be taken off the shelf at any time, removed from its can, sliced and served. The Hormel Meatpacking Company had been selling canned ham for some time, but could not market the shoulder. In 1937 Jay Hormel had the idea of combining shoulder and ham in a convenient-sized can; soon its name of spiced ham was changed to the catchier Spam.

Spam. This pork shoulder loaf is nicer when fried. Some enthusiasts make it into elaborate dishes.

Spam came into its own in the Second World War because it was cheap and easily transportable and had an indefinite shelf life. Therefore it was practical both for feeding soldiers and for shipping overseas to aid foreign countries. By 1944, 90 per cent of Hormel's Spam went to American soldiers, who might get it twice a day, and to overseas civilians. It was prized in Italy and England. And no wonder – it must have been a godsend to people who had no or substandard meat. Many meats are much less appetizing than fried slices of Spam. Nikita Khrushchev said Spam tasted 'good' and wrote that, 'Without Spam we wouldn't have been able to feed our army.' American soldiers were less appreciative, calling it 'ham that didn't pass its physical' and 'meat loaf without basic training'.[10] Nonetheless, they became familiar with Spam in the army and many of them grew to love it; its sales increased after the Second World War. Although its sales are not as strong as they were 30 or 40 years ago, they are still solid; Spam retains a loyal following. It now exists in ten varieties, some responding to health concerns (Spam Lite and Spam Low Sodium) or interest in more exotic tastes (Spam Hickory Smoked and Spam Hot & Spicy).

Spam is a prized meat in Hawaii and has become incorporated into the Japanese-influenced cuisine: not only is it served in ramen noodle soup and bento boxes, but Spam sushi – a roll made of sticky rice placed on a slice of fried Spam and wrapped in seaweed – is a universal take-out snack. In Guam, where American troops were stationed during the Second World War, the annual per capita consumption of Spam is 8 pounds (3.6 kilograms). Sam Choy, a prominent chef and restaurateur in Hawaii, proudly invented Pineapple Spam, made by simmering together cubes of Spam and pineapple with soy sauce, sliced ginger and a large amount of brown sugar. Hormel developed recipes, of which the most notable was Spam glazed with brown sugar and studded with cloves like a baked ham. The company also inspired American housewives to create Planked Spam, baked on a plank, garnished with a rim of mashed potatoes, grilled tomato halves and parsley; or Spam 'N' Yam Fiesta Loaf, seasoned canned sweet potatoes sandwiched between slices of Spam, garnished with canned peach slices, drizzled with the peach juice spiked with mustard, and baked for 30 minutes. Spam's website currently displays the prizewinning Torte Rustica Appetizer (thinly sliced Spam layered with cheese, spinach, roasted peppers and Italian seasoning between two sheets of puff pastry) and Spam Fideo (browned Spam cubes mixed with fideo pasta, canned peas and canned corn).

From the beginning, pigs particularly thrived in the southern states of America, where the mild winters made it possible for them to forage outside all year long; and pork has a special place in Southern cooking. Although fresh pork was available only in the winter, pork is good when preserved, and lard keeps better than butter. The best American hams came from the South, particularly from around Smithfield, Virginia. There the local pigs foraged in the woods during the summer, eating nuts and roots, and in the autumn gleaned the harvested peanut fields; finally they were confined and corn-fed until slaughtering time. Although these pigs no longer run free, their hams are still prepared in the traditional way. They are rubbed with salt, nitrate and sometimes sugar or pepper, and stored in a cool, dark area for four weeks. Then they are washed, hung up in a net bag, and aged for anything from six months to years. Hickory or other hardwood smoke may be wafted into the ageing barn. Virginia ham was so valued that an early colonial governor used to send his home-cured hams home to his brother and three other bishops in England, and Queen Victoria placed a standing order for Virginia hams. These hams must be soaked in water overnight, scrubbed to remove their layer of mould, and simmered for about five hours. After cooking, they may be glazed and baked or fried in slices. Red-eye gravy, made by browning a slice of ham with plenty of fat and deglazing the pan with boiling black coffee, may be poured over the meat. 'Ham biscuits', little sandwiches made by putting slivers of country ham into American-style biscuits with chutney and mustard, are standard party food in the South.

As Frederick Douglass Opie says, whites in the South 'may have eaten high on the hog while blacks ate low, but they both ate from the same hog . . . The hog . . . was fed with Indian corn.'[11] ('Living high on the hog', meaning living well, is another metaphor that shows the prominence of pork in American culture. The most desirable cuts of pork – loin, tenderloin, and ham – come from the upper part of the pig's

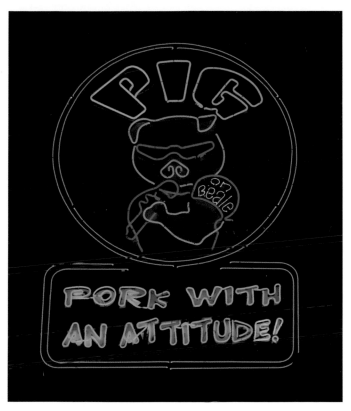

Pig neon sign, Beale Street, Memphis, Tennessee.

body, while the lower part yields spare ribs, once a cheap cut, bacon, salt pork and trotters.) Slaves received a daily ration of salt pork, and some were able to raise pigs on their own plots. A relatively generous plantation owner in Alabama in the 1830s gave each slave weekly four pounds (1.8 kg) of bacon, a peck (a volume measurement equivalent to nine litres) of cornmeal, a pint of molasses, three salted fish, a supply of fresh meat when available, and all the vegetables they wanted. (Molasses was a welcome corrective to the salty taste of cured pork.) At hog-killing time, the slaves got the less desirable parts, and they learned to make the most of them. They used hog maws, trotters, hog jowl, ham hocks and neck bones to flavour their black-eyed peas (beans), yams, collard or turnip greens, and corn bread. They fried the chitterlings, and moistened fried salt pork with cream gravy. They baked a mixture of cornmeal and water on a griddle, fried thin slices of salt pork until crisp, added molasses to the fat and ate them together. Or they might make crackling bread by mixing cracklings from rendering lard with cornmeal, salt, soda and buttermilk, and baking it brown. In North and South America, cracklings are typically produced, not on roast pork as in Britain, but by rendering pork fat.

It is said that stuffed ham, a Maryland speciality often featured at Easter, was originally developed by slaves, who had to work with the relatively undesirable pig's head. They made fifteen to twenty deep slits in the head and stuffed them with a mixture of kale, cabbage, spinach, spring onions and pepper. The combination of sweet pork and peppery greens was so good that more prosperous people adopted it, using a ham instead of the head. After soaking and simmering for an hour, the rind and most of the fat are cut off, the incisions are made and stuffed, and the whole is wrapped tightly in cheesecloth and simmered for three to four hours. The ham is thinly sliced and served at room temperature.

Reporting from North Carolina in 1940, Katherine Palmer described a 'Chitlin (Chitterling) Strut', a festive fundraiser among African Americans. When Mehitable and Doak Dorsey butchered their hogs in late autumn and put the chitlins to soak in salt water, they spread the word among the local black population, who came dressed up and each gave Doak 25 cents at the door. Mehitable cooked the chitlins, a lengthy, laborious process:

> You got to get yore chitlins clean and sweet . . . Them
> chitlins been done fussed with right smart. After the hawgs
> is kilt and scraped and the chitlins took out, I squeezes
> them chitlins clean as I can with my hands. Then I washes
> them through two waters. Then I cuts them open length-
> wise and washes them two more times, then I scrapes 'em
> good and plenty with a dull knife. After that I washes
> them in two more waters and they is ready for the salt-
> water soakin. After soakin . . . two days they is boiled three
> hours . . . After they soaks in salt water I rinses 'em good
> ag'in, and cuts 'em in fo-inch lengths, and rolls 'em in
> meal, and I fries 'em in medium fat. Hawg lard's the
> bestest . . . Some likes 'em [crisp and] brown, some likes
> 'em medium, and some likes 'em jes warmed through.[12]

She adds no flavouring, depending on the natural taste; the
sour flavour of vinegar, for example, would spoil the taste.
Coleslaw, pickles, molasses, corn bread and coffee are also
served. Dinner is followed by a dance.

Chitterlings might also be boiled, served cold with vinegar and red pepper sauce or hot with barbecue dressing.
Whatever the recipe, it is obviously essential that they be long
and carefully washed under cold running water. The Sterns
describe buying a batch of chitterlings, the local speciality,
that smelled so appalling they had to be flung out of the car
untouched.

A skilled cook could make a tasty diet from the cheap
ingredients available. Cured pork can be a very effective flavour
booster. One African American woman recalled from her
childhood in Alabama:

> Turnip, mustard, and collard greens glistened with a few
> slivers of ham hocks and so did crowder peas and butter

beans. A meaty ham bone was simmered with potatoes and green beans or with tomatoes, rice, corn, and okra for delicious stews.

But a diet consisting of pork three times a day with everything fried could be both unpalatable and unwholesome. A recipe for 'ol' cabin cabbage' suggests what this cuisine could degenerate to: boil cabbage with a hunk of meat (that is, fat pork) 'till you can't tell the meat from the cabbage and the cabbage from the meat'.[13]

Traditional African American cooking came to be called soul food as black pride developed in the 1960s and '70s: dishes created to make the most of cheap ingredients became a prized part of their culture. Black people could now take pride in their food and write soul food cookbooks that inspired white people to imitate it. Perhaps the single most important characteristic of soul food is its pervasive use of pork, not only in itself but for flavouring greens and deep-frying fish and chicken. The cooking liquid for pork and greens, 'pot likker', is enthusiastically drunk like soup, with corn bread. Some modern African Americans renounce soul food for its effect on health (as well as, in the case of the Nation of Islam, for religious reasons), but it is rightly prized, not only because it is traditional, but because it produces very tasty food at very little cost.

Like Europeans, Americans from all regions used pork to enhance the cheap nutrition provided by beans. Hoppin' John, made in the West Indies and the American South, consists of cowpeas or black-eyed peas cooked with fat pork, to which raw rice is added halfway through, seasoned with salt, pepper and onion. It is traditionally served on New Year's Day to bring good luck for the year. The New Orleans version uses red beans and more seasonings. Traditionally it is made with the bone of Sunday's ham, together with any meat or fat leftovers. Paul Prudhomme explains that on Monday the housewife 'could put on a pot of beans to cook and then get on with her washing while the beans simmered for hours with little or no attention. When the washing was done, the beans were ready to eat.'[14] Red beans and rice can now be presented as an elegant dish, as when Craig Claiborne adds ham steak, tomato paste, and chorizo to the beans and ham bone. In Haitian *Riz et Pois Colles*, the red beans are cooked with the rice and flavoured with salt pork, onion, spring onions and parsley. Cuba has *Moros y Cristianos*, black beans with ham or fried salt pork, seasonings, and vegetables cooked into a sauce that is poured over rice, and *Lentejas con Puerco*, lentils cooked with browned pork cubes and garnished with bananas. In Brazil, the slaves enhanced their rations of black beans, jerked beef and rice with spices and discarded pig parts like tongues, ears, feet and tails, as well as greens, to create *feijoada*, now the national dish.

The Puritan settlers of New England baked pea or navy beans with salt pork and flavoured them with dry mustard, salt and molasses. Because this dish could be prepared on Saturday evening and left in the oven overnight, it saved them from having to cook on the Sabbath. Baked beans remain a classic American dish. Little pots of beans topped with bits of crisp pork fat were one of the most popular items at the Horn and Hardart Automats in Philadelphia and New York, which featured wholesome traditional American budget food and flourished from 1902 through the 1960s.

Cattle were more demanding to keep than pigs, and in the early days they were kept for milk rather than beef. By the late nineteenth century, however, a major cattle industry had emerged in the American West, and railways with refrigerated cars could transport cattle and beef all around the country.

In 1909, for the first time, America produced more beef than pork products. And by the same year, northern urban whites were eating more beef than pork, southern urban whites were eating the same amount of each, and northern blacks almost the same. Only Southern blacks continued clearly to prefer pork. At the same time, pork came to be associated with the lower classes. In the 1880s the editor of *The Home-maker* magazine commented that any who had seen how pigs lived and were fed 'cannot marvel at the growing prejudice against pork in all its varieties that pervades our best classes'.[15] Mary Hinman Abel, writing a cookbook for 'persons of moderate and small means' (1890), reluctantly admitted that pork was valuable, but only because of its low cost.[16] Even so, Juliet Corson, superintendent of the New York Cooking School, made less use of pork than one might expect when she suggested menus for a week in her *Fifteen Cent Dinners for Workingmen's Families* (1877) and *Twenty-five Cent Dinners for Families of Six* (1885). About half the dinner menus in the first book are based on pork, as contrasted to only two of seven in her book for slightly more prosperous people. Her pork recipes reveal more concern for thrift than interest in taste appeal – salt pork and cabbage stew, pig's organ stew (liver, heart and lungs), pig's brain and liver pudding. Elizabeth Hillyer, another domestic science teacher, recommended pork even less often in *52 Sunday Dinners: A Book of Recipes* (1915), addressed to the middle class. Of her 52 suggested menus for the best dinner of each week, only four feature pork, all prime cuts and all roasted: roast shoulder and roast loin, baked ham and Pork Tenderloin Lyonnaise.

Miss Eliza Leslie, in her *New Cookery Book* (1857) declared that bacon, meaning any smoked pork except the ham, 'is too plain a dish for any but a country table'. But she considered ham 'a delicacy for the city, or for any place'.[17] Curiously, ham was more prestigious than fresh pork, probably because people suspected that pork kept less well than other meats. Leslie's disdain for pork was, however, modified by her evident recognition of the practical fact that it is an economical meat and therefore worth painstaking cooking. She gave directions for roasting the best cuts of fresh pork, as well as two ways of serving baked ham. She also included economy recipes – for leftovers, sausages and pigs' feet.

Fannie Merritt Farmer, who attended the Boston Cooking School and eventually ran it, published her first *Boston Cooking-School Cook Book* in 1896; this became the most influential of all American cookbooks. It has been a constant bestseller and went into its thirteenth revised edition in 1990 (by Marion Cunningham). Farmer, a proponent of scientific cookery, did not approve of pork. She lent her authority to the idea, common in the nineteenth century, that pork is an unhealthy indulgence. Following Sarah Josepha Hale, an authority on housewifery who had warned that 'a full meal of roast pork . . . is a hazardous experiment' that will 'cause heaviness and nausea' to any but the strongest stomach, Farmer said that fresh pork is of all meats

> the most difficult of digestion, and . . . it should be but seldom served, and then only during the winter months. By curing, salting, and smoking, pork is rendered more wholesome.

Beef, on the other hand, 'is the most nutritious and largely consumed of all animal foods'.[18] She includes remarkably few pork recipes – fifteen, as compared to 50 for beef and veal, 23 for lamb and mutton, and 32 for chicken. The pork recipes are for plainly cooked pork chops, roast and tenderloin, breakfast bacon, fried salt pork with codfish, broiled

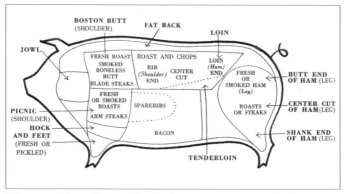

Diagram of the main cuts of pork, from a contemporary American cookbook.

ham slice, fried ham and eggs, boiled ham, roast ham with champagne sauce, Westphalian ham (simply sliced), broiled and fried breaded pigs' feet, plain fried sausages, and baked beans with salt pork. Her long list of soups includes pork only in four of her chowders. Chowders – thick soups made of clams, corn or potatoes – are generally started by browning diced salt pork and adding liquid and the main ingredients to the melted fat. Pork appears in only two of her elaborate breakfast menus (bacon and eggs, broiled ham) in one of her eighteen luncheon menus (broiled ham, again), and not in a single dinner menu (three beef main dishes, six fish, four poultry, four lamb and one veal). Nor is there a pork dish in any of her three formal (twelve-course) dinners.

As would be expected, pork seldom appeared at Delmonico's, a pre-eminent New York restaurant of the period. Charles Ranhofer, a chef at Delmonico's, did include pork recipes, including recipes for salt pork, pigs' feet and other unfashionable parts, in his *The Epicurean: A Complete Treatise . . . on the Culinary Art* (1893). But pork practically never appears in the 86 menus he provides for special dinners given at

Delmonico's, even though each dinner included multiple dishes. It is used only in side dishes – Westphalian ham and galantine of suckling pig in one dinner, boudins in another and fried ham in a third. It is never once featured as a main roast.

Marion Cunningham, revising Farmer's *Boston Cooking-School Cook Book* in 1979 and again in 1990, gives more attention to pork, but still reveals the American preference for beef: she provides 55 beef and veal recipes and 36 pork (including fresh pork, ham and sausage). She includes recipes for pigs' feet and inner organs, as well as the prime cuts. She drops the old belief that pork is unhealthy, pointing out that it is 'high in protein and in vitamin B1', as well as flavourful. And she reflects the increasing interest of Americans in diverse and exotic recipes – besides the conventional roast pork loin and pork chops with various accompaniments, there is a Chinese-style dish marinated and baked in a mixture of hoisin sauce, ketchup, sugar, sherry and soy sauce. She revives City Chicken – pork and chicken cubes threaded on skewers, breaded, browned and simmered in sauce, which dates back to 'Depression days, when chicken was more expensive than pork'.[19]

Although Cunningham offers a wide range of pork and ham recipes and indicates the multiple uses of pork and ham in flavouring soups, chicken, vegetables and pasta, she makes little use of pork in her suggested menus. Only one of her eight family dinners features pork – a picnic ham (smoked pork shoulder) – while there are three beef main dishes (and two chicken, one fish and one lamb). Each of her small dinner parties features some other meat or fish. In all these American cookbooks there is an odd discrepancy between the number of pork and ham recipes offered, indicating the continuing popularity of this meat, and the infrequency with which it is proposed as the main course.

Changing American tastes are revealed by the food expenditures of two professional families in 1816–17 and in 1926–7. The earlier family spent about the same percentage of its meat budget on pork as on beef, but five-sixths of that pork was cured. The 1926 family spent considerably more on beef than pork – 49.7 per cent of their meat budget on beef and 39.3 per cent on pork – and about half the pork they bought was fresh (reflecting the introduction of refrigeration). The 1916 family spent 0.7 per cent of its total food budget on lard; the 1926 family, only 0.1 per cent. (These figures must be interpreted in the light of significantly higher prices for beef than pork.) In 1950 Americans ate on average 57 pounds (25.9 kg) of beef per person, 64 (29 kg) of pork, and four (1.8 kg) of lamb and mutton; in 1970, 86 pounds of beef, 55 of pork, and three of lamb; in 1994, 64 pounds of beef, 50 of pork and one of lamb. In 2000 Americans averaged 64.5 pounds (29.3 kg) of beef per person (down 30 per cent from peak consumption in the 1970s) and 53 pounds (24 kg) of chicken, which had become an economy meat after the Second World War. Pork was the third most popular meat, at 47.7 pounds (21.6 kg) per person. The average for fish was fifteen pounds (6.8 kg) per person, and lamb only one.[20]

In the US, as in Great Britain, the most highly prized meat is beef, especially in the form of steak or roast beef. In a Gallup poll of 1947, most Americans chose steak as the main item in their ideal meal. In 1962 the most popular TV dinners were fried chicken, roast turkey, Salisbury steak and roast beef. Hamburgers have taken over the fast-food industry. The earliest drive-in restaurant in the US, which flourished in the 1920s and '30s, was the 'Pig Stand' in Texas, which specialized in the 'Pig Sandwich' – pork loin, pickle relish and barbecue sauce in a bun. But today's McDonald's menu offers only one pork spare rib burger and one bacon and cheese wrap among twelve beef hamburgers, eight chicken burgers, three beef wraps, six chicken wraps and one fish burger. Only bacon and other forms of cured pork retain their popularity. Most of McDonald's breakfast dishes feature ham, sausage or bacon. Bacon often garnishes hamburgers and is the key ingredient of the universal bacon, lettuce and tomato sandwich. Italian sausages, once confined to Italian immigrant communities, are now commonly sold off street carts in sausage and pepper sandwiches, and in fast-food restaurants as toppings for pizza.

Beef is preferred in some parts of Latin America, but pork is the favourite meat in the Caribbean and the Andean countries. *Chicharrones*, crisply fried cracklings, are a very popular street snack around the Caribbean. Families in San Juan, Puerto Rico, often drive out on Sunday afternoons to a nearby road called La Ruta del Lechón, because it is lined with roadside cafeterias serving luscious roast suckling pig. Roast suckling pig or baked ham is generally the centrepiece of Christmas dinner in that part of the world. Cubans are fond of marinated roast pork and pressed Cuban sandwiches

Mexican *chicharron carnudo*, a delicacy of fried pork skin.

filled with ham, pork, cheese and a pickle. Pigs' feet fritters, long simmered and then deep-fried, are a popular appetizer in Ecuador. It was traditional in rural Ecuador to celebrate a festive occasion by killing a pig and spending the day eating its parts: first cracklings, then fried chunks of pork, and in the evening sausages and soup made with the pig's inner organs.

5
Pork in the Far East

Pork has never lost its place as the favourite meat in China. Indeed, in China 'meat' means pork unless otherwise specified. 'Meat fried rice' is assumed to contain pork; otherwise it would be called 'chicken' or 'beef' fried rice. Most Chinese would rather eat pork than beef because cattle are working animals in China, and the people do not think it right to eat the animal that works so hard to help farmers, in the same way that many Europeans would object to eating horses. Cattle did not exist in herds in China, but rather as individual animals that made it possible for a farmer to feed the nation. Pigs, on the other hand, do nothing for their owners except provide food. It is relevant, of course, that China does not have a lot of pasture land for grazing. A pig can be kept in a small space or left to scavenge on its own. The Chinese character for *home* is made by putting the character for *roof* over the character for *pig*, suggesting that historically a typical family would have a pig that would live around or even in its house. In striking contrast to those who loathe the pig as unclean, the Chinese find its meat and fat more appetizing in colour and smell and easier to digest than other red meat.

Long ago, deforestation and high population density in China made it impossible for pigs to forage at large. They were kept in pens and as 'privy pigs' were used to process human waste. A family of four could sustain four young pigs on their own waste plus garbage. Since they did not range at large, Chinese pigs became smaller and fatter than their counterparts in the West. In the mid-eighteenth century English landowners improved the succulence of their pigs by crossing them with the small, plump, short-legged Chinese pigs. The resultant breed, the Large White (called the Yorkshire in the US), became the most popular breed in the world. It is long and relatively lean, and its pink skin shows through sparse white hair. It was originally bred to produce bacon, but now is especially valued because of the preference for lean pork. Most market pigs, however, are the product of crossing breeds. Niman Ranch, a large association of family farmers in the US, favours a hybrid of Large White, Chester White, Hampshire and Duroc pigs.

Food stall in Hong Kong.

In 2009 China consumed over half the world's supply of pork, partly, of course, because there are so many Chinese. The per capita consumption of pork is almost as high in China as it is in the European Union and probably would be higher if the standard of living there were the same as in Europe. Pork comprises the largest part of a total meat intake that is small by our standards. Peasants might have braised and fried pork dishes at a wedding feast. Red-braised pork was the favourite dish of Mao Zedong, who came from a prosperous Hunan peasant family. More often, poor people use a bit of fresh or smoked pork to flavour a vegetable dish. During the worst days of Mao's regime, they made do by rubbing pieces of pork fat around their woks to give their vegetables a hint of meaty flavour, afterwards putting the fat away so they could use it again. A working-class family in Hong Kong (whose diet was described for 1974–5) got most of their protein from fish. Meat was always pork in small amounts, in the form of fresh meat or dry salami-like sausage. They might have pieces of chicken for a company dinner and a whole chicken for a major festival, but there would also be large servings of pork. Chicken appeared at nineteen of the meals observed, pork at 79.

While pork and ham appear occasionally as the main dish in a Western meal, Chinese families that can afford meat serve pork at nearly every meal. New Year's dinner is not complete without at least one traditional pork dish, and perhaps fresh ham, ground pork and cabbage dumplings, pig's-feet jelly and the giant pork meatballs known as lions' heads would all be served. Prosperous people generally have several dishes plus one staple food at lunch and dinner, with one of the dishes including pork. As in the West, pork is commonly used to add flavour to sauces and vegetables, although the Chinese generally use fresh pork rather than the bacon or ham more usual in the West.

Chinese farmers
sell their goods
at market, Dali,
2010.

While Europeans and Americans typically eat fresh pork in the form of loin roasts and fried chops, Chinese cooks generally shred or cube it and stir-fry it with vegetables and sauce. Food cooks more quickly if it is cut into small pieces, and fuel has always been scarce in China. Stir-frying with other ingredients provides opportunities to exploit textural contrasts within a dish – crisp carrots and bamboo shoots, for example, contrasting with the rich succulence of pork strips. Stir-frying is fast, easily varied and economical, making it possible to combine a pound of meat with other ingredients so as to serve six or seven people. It is important that the ingredients be chopped in uniform sizes, so that they look neat and take the same amount of time to cook, and that the cooking be very quick. Traditionally, the Chinese 'don't eat with knives in [their] hands',[1] so meat must be cut up small (or, usually only for banquets, cooked to the point that it can be pulled apart with chopsticks). Pork may be 'red-cooked' – slowly simmered in a soy-sauce-based liquid – or 'twice-cooked' – parboiled and then sliced and fried till crisp. 'Twice-cooking' was originally devised for practical reasons; since boiled meat keeps better than fresh, large cuts were boiled and then carved as needed to make other dishes. Or pork may be deep-fried, steamed, white-cooked (slow-cooked in seasoned water, without soy sauce), ground and used in fillings or sausages, or dried and salted to produce a garnish for rice.

The Chinese fully appreciate all parts of a pig. An attentive Chinese host will make sure that his guests share the delights of pig intestine or brains. Pigs' feet are red-cooked, stewed, braised, chilled in aspic, pickled in vinegar or cooked

Chinese broccoli with crispy pork.

in soups. Pig's ear is cooked, shredded and served cold with a spicy dressing. The brain is deep-fried in batter. Much skill and effort is expended to turn kidneys into *Huo bao yao hua*, fire-exploded kidney flowers. First the kidneys are marinated in wine to eliminate the uriney taste. Then they are carefully cut two-thirds through with numerous parallel and perpendicular slashes, so that when they are rapidly cooked in fiery-hot oil, they curl up into frilly little morsels that no longer look like kidneys at all.

Pigs' lard is as important as their meat, and they are bred both for maximal fat content and maximal separation of fat and lean meat – that is, the opposite of our prized marbled beef. In Fukien, lard is widely used for cooking instead of the oil that is usual in Asia, because it is a mountainous area, with much fodder for pigs and little land on which to raise oilseeds.

Superior stock, made of pork and chicken bones and meat, using almost twice as much pork as chicken, is the basis of most soups and many other dishes. Hot and sour soup, especially popular in the north of China, features a small amount of shredded pork, simmered in the finished broth. Fukien meat wool is strips of pork simmered with seasonings for two hours, then baked in a slow oven for one hour, then fried very gently in lard for two hours. The object is to evaporate all the water from the meat. The result is extremely tasty dried meat, which is used to flavour congee, the rice porridge that forms the traditional Chinese breakfast. Pork is used to make sauce for noodles and to flavour vegetables such as green beans and aubergine (eggplant). It is ground with vegetables to stuff buns and dumplings. *Xiao long bao* is made by enclosing a filling of seasoned minced pork belly in a thin wrapper of dough made with pork fat and boiling the dumpling in a rich broth made from pork skin long boiled in stock; the result is a dumpling imbued with fatty deliciousness. *Dim sum*,

Shopkeeper selling *bakk wa*, Chinatown, Singapore. *Bakk wa*, or 'barbecue meat', is thin sheets of cured and dried pork.

the snacks served with tea, include roast pork pie, Chinese sausage buns, wonton skins filled with minced pork, steamed ribs in black bean sauce, steamed roast pork buns, barbecued ribs and pieces of roast suckling pig.

Pork dishes can be simple: for pork with bean sprouts, a cup of shredded pork is briefly marinated with soy sauce, sherry, MSG and cornstarch, then stir-fried with salt and a spring onion (scallion); four cups of bean sprouts are then added, and the whole is fried for an additional minute or two. Or pork dishes can be elaborate, such as sweet and sour pork, which is very popular in Canton and in the West as well. Introduced by the Cantonese cooks who were the first to settle in America, it may now be eaten more often in America than in Canton. Chinese-American sweet and sour pork tends to be sweeter and more heavily coated than in China. An authentic Cantonese recipe starts with lightly pickling cut-up carrots. Then pork cubes are marinated in wine and soy sauce, coated with egg yolk, dredged in cornflour (cornstarch) and left to air-dry. Then they are deep-fried in batches and drained, after which they get another minute of frying and are drained again. Then green pepper pieces are stir-fried with garlic, and the carrots and pineapple chunks are added. Finally, the vegetables are covered with a sauce flavoured with ketchup, vinegar, soy sauce, sesame oil, sugar and salt; and the pork is replaced and heated. Medallions of pork with crabmeat filling consists of little squares of roasted pork loin spread with a mixture of finely chopped crabmeat, mushrooms and bamboo shoots; these are topped with more pork squares, and the resulting sandwiches are dipped in egg white and deep fat fried. Dishes may have wonderfully colourful names: seasoned fried ground pork sauce over bean thread noodles is called 'Ants Climbing a Tree', because the bits of pork cling to the noodles on your chopsticks like ants clinging to the twigs of a tree.

Just as in the West, the Chinese cured parts of a slaughtered pig to preserve them. Their most famous ham is Yunnan

Pork leg stew over rice (*kao ka moo*).

ham, which is hard and dry-cured, much like American Smithfield ham. Chinese cooks use ham principally as a seasoning or a garnish, shredding it for egg dishes or stir fries, rather than serving it as a main meat in slices or chunks. Chinese sausage, pungent and sweeter than Western varieties, will keep indefinitely in a cool place. The proportion of fat to meat is high, and the particles of each are larger than in European sausages. There are over twenty types, some requiring cooking and some ready to eat. One recipe calls for 1½ pounds of pork fat to 2 pounds of lean, cut into ¼-inch (1-cm) cubes and seasoned with sugar, soy sauce and spices. It is marinated, then stuffed into casings and refrigerated for two or three days, after which it must be fried or steamed before eating. There is no Chinese equivalent to bacon, although pork belly may be cured, in which case it tastes like our bacon.

The Chinese attribute high importance to food. Confucius himself decreed in his *Analects* that meat should be neither under- nor overcooked, should be appropriately seasoned, cut straight and served with its proper sauce. One famous pork dish is named for Su Dongpo, a great poet of the Song Dynasty. (Can you imagine William Wordsworth Beef?) According to tradition, while the poet was serving as governor of Hangzhou, he invented the dish to reward the labourers who had built a dam or causeway under his direction. It consists of pork belly, complete with skin and lots of fat, cooked long and slowly until the skin and fat become jelly-like and the meat is meltingly tender. One version involves marinating the pork in wine, soy sauce, ginger, spring onion (scallion) and garlic; baking the meat and marinade with onions and a bit of stock for two hours and fifteen minutes; then vigorously steaming the pork pieces with their gravy for fifteen minutes. Another simmers the pork in water, then braises it in water, soy sauce and other seasonings, then takes it from the sauce and fries it, then replaces it in the sauce to simmer for thirty minutes, and finally steams it over spring onions for two hours.

Pork spread from China through South-east Asia and the Pacific Islands. It remains popular in South-east Asia, except where the people have converted to Islam. Pork is the favoured meat in Vietnam, although it is rarely available to the poorer class. Pigs roam through the villages, foraging during the day and running home in the evening when called to their supper of more scraps. As in China, pork is typically used in small quantities, often just to flavour soup, vegetables or salads. Dishes such as Vietnamese shrimp and pork stir fry or sliced pork with long beans use very little meat by Western standards – a half-pound (225 g) or less for two to four people. Vietnamese grilled pork balls, made of marinated pork ground with pork fat, are prepared all over Vietnam – in restaurants, street stalls and homes. They are served on rice or noodles or with a herb and salad plate and a dipping sauce of lime juice and fish sauce. *Banh chung*, steamed rice cakes stuffed with pork, sweet bean paste and fish sauce, are always served during the Tet holiday in Vietnam. Breakfast for the middle class typically includes a minced pork broth with rice noodles.

The Thais have a distinctive sausage, *Si Klok*, made of equal parts of shredded crabmeat and of ground pork and fat, flavoured with coriander leaves, fish sauce, coconut milk, chilli paste, galingal, ground peanuts and garlic. The combination of pork with seafood is typical, since Thais eat more seafood than meat, and is also seen in such dishes as pork and shrimp toast or fried prawns stuffed with ground pork filling. Pork is generally included, along with other meat and seafood, in fried rice. To preserve pork in villages without refrigeration, the Thais invented *Moo Wan*, their equivalent of ham. They simmer pork loin or butt with sugar, fish sauce

Food stall in Yangon, Myanmar.

and water, and reboil it daily. This may be served in its own reduced sauce or, more usually, cut up in fried rice or other dishes. Pork is by far the most widely eaten meat in Laos and Burma. The national dish of Laos is *Khao Poon*, an elaborate pork and noodle dish served in a piquant sauce.

Spanish influence doubtless contributed to the popularity of pork in the Philippines. *Jamon de Navidad*, a baked ham glazed with brown sugar and fruit, or *lechon de leche*, charcoal-roasted suckling pig, is the centrepiece of Christmas and Easter dinner in the Philippines. Pork, sometimes combined with chicken, is the basis of *Adobo*, the national stew; in one typical version, the meat is marinated in vinegar, soy sauce, garlic, peppercorns and tamarind paste, then simmered until the liquid evaporates, and then browned in lard with soy sauce; fried onions and Chinese cabbage may be added. It is eaten both at everyday meals and feasts, and, because the vinegar preserves it without refrigeration, is practical for taking

Pig at a *luau*, a traditional Hawaiian meal in which a whole pig may be roasted in a barbecue pit.

along on journeys. Dinuguan is a pork stew that uses up the blood and internal organs, the by-products of a pig butchering, and is widely served at any meal or snack.

Bali, one of the few areas in Indonesia that is not mainly Muslim, is known for its pork dishes. Balinese coconut pork, lean pork cooked in seasoned coconut milk, combines Hindu spices with the coconut milk characteristic of South-east Asia. In Melanesia pigs occupy a special position, similar to that of dogs in the West, even though they are eaten. Unlike other animals, they are believed to have souls something like ours. They are groomed and trained and often allowed to suckle at a woman's breast. They roam during the day and are called in at sunset, when they eagerly come in to be scratched and rubbed. When they grow large, they are kept in pens. Eventually, but only on some special occasion, they are slaughtered in a ritual sacrifice and become a feast for the village. The apparent contradiction between expressing affection and respect for an animal and nevertheless eating it seems less incongruous when we recall that until recently Melanesians ate humans, presumably with the same ambivalence.

People in diverse cultures have said that human meat tastes like pork, and Polynesian cannibals referred to human meat as 'long pig'. Anthony Burgess, working for the British government in New Guinea shortly after the Second World War, took some meat at a ceremonial feast that tasted 'very much like a fine, delicately sweet pork, which is what I thought it was. When I was told that it was the meat from enemy warriors who had been killed in a recent tribal skirmish I almost immediately . . . threw up.'[2] Polynesian voyagers took pigs with them everywhere they went, and a whole pit-roasted pig is the centrepiece of a *luau*, their ceremonial feast. A pit is dug in the earth and filled with rocks, which are heated red hot; the gutted pig is put in, along with fish and vegetables; the pit is covered with layers of wet leaves and earth; and the food is slowly cooked by the heat of the rocks.

6
Today's Mass-produced Pork

Today we can go into a supermarket and find neatly packaged pork chops, pork loins, salt pork, bacon, precooked ham and sausages of various kinds. The bacon is conveniently sliced, the whole or half ham needs only to be heated for a couple of hours in the oven, the sausages are ready to fry or serve without cooking. Saving of time and labour is even more apparent in pork production in the factory. Ham and bacon are no longer dry-cured. Rather, brine is injected into a ham so that it is cured in five to ten days. The resulting hams may be bland and waterlogged, but processing more hams in less time saves money. Bacon is made by plunging thousands of pounds of pork sides into vats of a solution of brine and various chemicals, to which liquid smoke and other flavourings are added. The traditional process, which was usual in Britain up to the First World War, involved rubbing the meat with dry salt and flavourings, leaving it to cure for days, and slow-smoking it over wood fires. This took six to eight weeks. Now practically all bacon is tank-cured in nine to ten days – submerged in brine for four to five days, then drained for four. Often ham and bacon are barely smoked at all. Without slow ageing, the intense flavour proper to cured pork does not have a chance to develop. Because they are not thoroughly cured, ham and bacon must be kept in sealed packages and refrigerated after they are opened. Fresh sausages are no longer mixed and seasoned to taste at home and stuffed into natural meat casings. At first the casings for mass-produced sausages were made of plastic; now at least they are made of edible collagen or cellulose.

Up-to-date slaughterhouses can process about a thousand pigs per hour. The animals are shooed onto a ramp leading to the killing floor, where they are stunned insensible by electrodes (or so we hope) and hoisted up by a hind leg to an overhead conveyor chain. There they are stuck in their carotid arteries and jugular vein so they bleed to death. The chain conveys them through a vat of $180°F/82°C$ water, then past mechanical brushes that whisk away all the bristles, then between vertical banks of blue flames that singe and harden the skin. The body is decapitated, slit down the centre and disembowelled, leaving a split, gutted carcass hanging by its hind leg. This all takes only minutes. From here the body is

British-style sausages on a grill.

Customers are beginning to demand that their meat be raised in a less intensive fashion, allowing for happier pigs.

conveyed to refrigeration rooms to be cut into parts. It is said that Henry Ford was inspired by Philip Danforth Armour's 'pig disassembly' line, organized in Chicago around 1875, to set up his assembly line for Model Ts.

Ford's metaphor takes on moral significance when we consider that pigs are 'assembled' on farms with similar efficiency. When pigs were raised on family farms, they foraged outside and, in bad weather, were sheltered in barns with plenty of straw bedding. Mrs Beeton's instructions on how to maintain a pig in 'health, cleanliness, and comfort' supply a favourable but not unrealistic description of the life of a farmer's pig in mid-nineteenth-century England. He should be kept in a sty with a constant supply of fresh water and given waste roots, stalks and leaves from the garden 'for the delectation of his leisure moments'. The front part of the sty should be floored with brick, sprinkled with sand, and swept

An early 20th-century poster of a woman feeding pigs at a trough. Pork producers cultivate an image of the idyllic life of pigs on traditional farms.

out every day. The rear, 'his lair, or sleeping apartment, should be well sheltered by roof and sides from cold, wet, and all changes of weather, and the bed made up of a good supply of clean straw, sufficiently deep' to burrow under.[1] It was not too bad a life.

In the past 50 to 100 years, however, pork producers, in North America, Australia and the European Union, and increasingly in Asia and South America, have shifted to a more profitable system that treats pigs as production units rather than sentient animals. Pork production has become a centralized industry, controlled by a few large corporations that contract with farmers, who themselves each keep thousands of pigs. These pigs spend their lives crowded into dimly lit metal or concrete warehouses with slatted or wire mesh floors to facilitate removal of excrement. After artificial insemination, pregnant sows are kept in gestation crates just big enough to hold their bodies, where they cannot even turn around; after giving birth they are kept in small farrowing crates with a grate between them and their litter, so the piglets can suckle from but not cuddle with their mother. (The partition prevents any possible losses from the sow's rolling over on her offspring as a result of the confined space.) The piglets are taken from their mother at three weeks, instead of the natural thirteen, because they gain weight faster on drug-fortified feed than on sow's milk. They are slaughtered at five to seven months, when they reach market weight of 220 to 280 pounds (100–127 kilograms).

But even so they are more fortunate than their mothers, who spend twelve years in gestation and farrowing crates (apart from a week's rest between pregnancies). Such practices prevail among all large-scale pork producers today. The National Pork Board of the United States lists animal well-being among its 'Ethical Principles for United States Pork

Top: Sows in gestation crates. These intelligent, curious animals spend most of their lives in crates where they can barely move. *Bottom*: Pigs spend months crowded in barren pens while awaiting slaughter; Farm Sanctuary, the USA's leading farm animal protection organization, promotes compassionate vegan living and believes that farm animals should not be exploited for commercial or other purposes. Learn more at: farmsanctuary.org.

Producers', and this includes 'an environment that promotes the well-being of our animals'. But the Board proceeds to point out the advantages of gestation crates. These, it claims, minimize aggression and competition among sows, make it easier to monitor their weight and safeguard the workers' safety. They are supposed to represent 'what is best for the pig', despite the evidently minor disadvantages of restriction of movement and exercise, incapacity to perform foraging behaviour and limitation of social interaction. The Board's website displays a series of genial film strips called *Food Comes from Farms*, in which an upstanding farmer explains that there are no windows in his pig barns because he takes care to give the animals just the light they need. He assures us that the crowd of pigs in their barren, slatted-floor warehouse are very comfortable and contented. Their tails have been docked to keep them from harming each other. He declares that his 750 sows in rows of gestation crates are relaxed and happy. The crates make it possible to care for them better, and they are artificially inseminated to protect them from the boar. This 'scientific method' is better for pigs as well as humans.

Fortunately, the smooth arguments have not convinced everyone. Public awareness and indignation have been aroused, and alternatives are beginning to appear. Gestation crates have been made illegal in the UK, Sweden and several states of the US. Since 2003 EU legislation has required that pigs must not be kept in a totally barren environment, but must have

> permanent access to a sufficient quantity of material to enable proper investigation and manipulation activities, such as straw, hay, wood . . . mushroom compost, peat, or a mixture of such.[2]

It also prohibits the routine tail-docking that is needed to minimize the aggression natural in highly confined quarters, and will phase out gestation crates. Unfortunately, however, investigators from the European Food Safety Authority discovered that these laws were being flouted by over half the farmers in the member countries. Under pressure from animal welfare groups, farmers in the American Midwest have reluctantly agreed to phase out gestation crates within fifteen years, although they see nothing wrong with them. Large pork producers in Australia have made a similar commitment. It can be argued that humanely farmed meat costs little more to produce than industrially farmed meat, because industrial farmers have to deal with pollution and infection: the crowded conditions on factory farms pollute the environment and necessitate dosing the animals with antibiotics to prevent the spread of disease. Probably, however, as long as the sole consideration is to produce the most pork in the least time with the lowest outlay of overhead and labour, factory farming is the most profitable method – as long as the factory farmers do not have to pay for controlling or cleaning up the pollution they cause.

Nevertheless, consumers in many countries are beginning to demand humanely raised meat, and farmers to provide it. Organizations such as Niwan Ranch, a network of over 650 independent American farmers, require their members to avoid routine use of antibiotics, to let their pigs forage, explore and play outside, to give them straw bedding and to let the sows build nests and care for their young. The owner of Polyface Farm in Virginia lets his pigs forage in the adjacent woodland, but he has also worked out a system based on their taste for alcohol (one of their eerie similarities to humans). He puts corn in the manure and straw that accumulate in his cow barn, which generates heat that ferments the corn. When the cows go out to pasture, he lets the pigs into the barn, and they eagerly root out the fermented corn. Thus they nourish and enjoy themselves and at the same time aerate the manure, turning it into sweet-scented compost. The pigs of Polyface Farm happily express their natural impulses at the same time that they grow fat for sale. Nineteenth-century peasants could not be expected to develop such elaborate systems, but generally their pigs lived good enough lives until the time came to repay the farmer for raising them.

Recipes

Pork Chops with Carrots

1 6 oz can frozen orange or pineapple-orange juice
3 tablespoons soy sauce
2 teaspoons ground ginger
½ teaspoon salt
½ teaspoon marjoram
3 thick pork chops
1 lb (450 g) carrots
2 tablespoons vegetable oil or fat cut from chops

Combine unthawed juice, soy sauce, ginger, salt and marjoram. Brown the chops well in the oil or fat. Pour on the juice mixture. Slice the carrots so they are ¼-inch (1-cm) thick and add to the pan. Simmer, stirring occasionally, for 30–45 minutes.
Serves 3

Pork Stew with Apples

Sally Grainger's adaptation of Apicius' *Matian minutal*, from *The Classical Cookbook* (London, British Museum Press, 1996)

1 lb (450 g) boned lean pork
3 tablespoons honey

1 bay leaf
5 peppercorns
1 celery stalk
8 oz (225 g) minced (ground) beef
1 small egg, beaten
1 large leek, sliced
1 large handful coriander, chopped
1 lb (450 g) small sweet apples, peeled and segmented
1¼ cup (280 ml) white wine
⅔ cup (150 ml) white wine vinegar
2 tablespoons olive oil
⅔ cup (150 ml) Thai fish sauce
2 teaspoons ground cumin
2 teaspoons ground coriander
1 teaspoon asafoetida
2 teaspoons chopped mint
cornflour (cornstarch) to thicken sauce
ground pepper

Simmer pork with water to cover, along with 1 tablespoon of the
honey, the bay leaf, peppercorns and celery stalk. Cool in its water.
Mix the beef and egg and form into small balls. In a separate bowl,
combine wine, 1¼ cups of the cooking liquid from the pork,
vinegar, olive oil, fish sauce and the remaining 2 tablespoons of
honey. Dice the pork and add it to this mixture, together with the
meatballs. Bring to a boil and add the leek, coriander and apple
slices. Simmer for 30 minutes, and add the cumin, ground coriander, asafoetida and mint when the pork is almost cooked. Thicken
the sauce with the cornflour and sprinkle generously with pepper.
Serves 4

Pork with Sauerkraut (Choucroute Garnie)

3 lbs/1.4 kg sauerkraut
2 slices bacon, chopped
1 cup minced onion
1 teaspoon minced garlic
1 bay leaf
6 juniper berries, crushed
½ teaspoon caraway seeds
½ cup (110 ml) white wine
½ cup (110 ml) chicken broth
pepper to taste
6 pork meatballs (recipe below)
1 lb (450 g) ham steak
1 lb (450 g) kielbasa, pricked

For the meatballs:
½ lb (225 g) ground pork
2½ tablespoons breadcrumbs
2½ tablespoons grated onion
½ tsp minced garlic
1¼ tablespoons sour cream
1¼ teaspoon minced parsley
salt and pepper
⅛ teaspoon nutmeg

Blend all the meatball ingredients, and shape into balls.

Drain and dry the sauerkraut and set aside. Fry bacon, add onion and garlic, and cook until wilted. Add the sauerkraut, bay leaf, juniper berries, caraway seeds, wine, broth and pepper. Bring to the boil. Add the meatballs, ham and kielbasa. Cover tightly and cook for one hour. Serve with boiled potatoes and mustard. Serves 6

Pot-roasted Pork with Prunes and Brandy

1 cup (225 ml) brandy
30 pitted medium prunes
4 lb (1.8 kg) boneless fresh ham
salt and pepper
¼ cup (60 ml) vegetable oil
2 red onions, cut into thick rounds
1 cup (225 ml) dry white wine
1 cup (225 ml) chicken stock (broth)
pinch of red pepper flakes
1 teaspoon dried sage (or 1 tablespoon fresh)
1 tablespoon tomato paste
¼ cup (60 ml) honey
2 tablespoons chopped parsley
½ cup (60 g) chopped toasted walnuts

Bring half of the brandy to a boil. Remove from the heat and add the prunes. Set aside. Preheat the oven to 325°F/ 160°C. Season the pork with salt and pepper, heat the oil in an ovenproof pot over a medium-high heat, and brown the pork on all sides (about 12 minutes in total). Remove the pork from the pan. Add the onions to the pot and cook over a medium heat until lightly browned (about 10 minutes), stirring occasionally. Add the white wine, remaining brandy, broth, red pepper flakes, sage, tomato paste and honey. Bring to the boil. Replace the pork in the pot, cover tightly with a lid or aluminum foil, and cook in the oven for 2 hours, until the pork is tender. Add the prunes with the brandy they were soaking in. Replace the pot in the oven, uncovered, for another 20 minutes. To serve, slice the pork and top with prunes, onions and some of the sauce. Garnish with the parsley and walnuts.
Serves 6

Shanghai Ham

4 lbs (1.8 kg) fresh ham, butt or shoulder
1 cup (225 ml) soy sauce
½ cup (100 g) sugar, or less
1 tablespoon dry sherry
2 slices fresh root ginger or 2 cloves garlic
a few cloves of star anise
1 cup (225 ml) water

Sear and scald the pork by soaking it in boiling water for a few minutes. Rinse with cold water. Place the pork and all the other ingredients in a large saucepan, bring to the boil, cover, and simmer, turning occasionally, until tender (about 2 hours or more). Uncover and increase the heat. Baste the pork until about 1 cup of liquid remains – another 15 or 20 minutes. Skim off the fat. Serve hot or cold.

Serves 6

Spaghetti Carbonara

1 lb (450 g) spaghetti
8 slices bacon, slivered
½ lb (225 g) ham, slivered
3 tablespoons butter
3 tablespoon extra-virgin olive oil
⅔ cup (60 g) Parmesan cheese, grated
1 tsp salt
1 tsp pepper
4 eggs
6 tablespoons parsley, chopped

Cook the spaghetti al dente. Meanwhile, brown the bacon in a large pan. Remove and drain, and pour off the fat. Sauté the ham slowly in the butter and oil for 4–5 minutes. Beat the eggs with the

Parmesan, salt and pepper. Remove the pan from the heat. Add the drained hot pasta, bacon, egg mixture and parsley. Toss to coat the spaghetti thoroughly, and serve at once.
Serves 5

Swedish Sausage Stew (*Koru Ragu*)

1 lb (450 g) fresh pork sausages
3 tablespoons butter
⅔ cup (80 g) chopped onion
1 tablespoon flour
1¼ cup (280 ml) beef stock (broth)
1¼ lb (600 g) potatoes, peeled and cut in small cubes
2½ cup (150 g) sliced carrots
1¼ teaspoon salt
½ teaspoon freshly ground black pepper
1 bay leaf

Lightly brown the sausages in a heavy pan. Remove, pour off the fat and reserve. Melt butter in the pan and sauté the onions for 5 minutes. Blend in the flour, then stir in the stock until the mixture boils. Add the sausages, potatoes, carrots, salt, pepper and bay leaf. Bring to a boil, cover, and cook over a low heat for 20 minutes.
Serves 5

Sweet and Sour Pork (*Gu Lu Rou*)

2 cups (120 g) carrots, cut in ¾ inch (2 cm) pieces
3 tablespoons rice vinegar
3 tablespoons sugar
3 quarter-size (10p-sized) slices of fresh root ginger, mashed
2 lbs (900 g) boneless pork loin

2 tablespoons rice wine
1½ tablespoons soy sauce
1 teaspoon sesame oil
2 egg yolks
2 cups cornstarch
2 cups peanut or corn oil
2 green peppers, cut into 1-inch pieces
1½ tablespoons garlic, minced
1 cup (175 g) pineapple chunks, drained

For the sauce, combine:
⅔ cup (150 ml) water
¼ cup (60 ml) ketchup
3 tablespoons vinegar
2 teaspoons soy sauce
½ teaspoon sesame oil
3 tablespoons sugar
2 teaspoons cornflour (cornstarch)
1 teaspoon salt

The night before, put the carrots in a mixture of 3 tablespoons of rice vinegar, 3 tablespoons of sugar and the mashed ginger. Marinate for 12 hours in the refrigerator, tossing occasionally.

On the day, when the carrots are ready to be used, remove the fat from the pork and cut it into 1-inch (2.5-cm) cubes. Marinate for at least 1 hour in a mixture of the wine, soy sauce and sesame oil. Remove the cubes, coat them with egg yolk, and dredge them in cornflour, lightly squeezing each piece to make sure the cornflour adheres. Place the cubes on a tray to air-dry for 1 hour. Heat a wok, add the peanut oil, and heat it to 400°F/200°C. Add one-third of the pork cubes, and deep fry for about 3 minutes, stirring constantly, until the meat is cooked and golden. Remove and drain. Reheat the oil, and fry the remaining pork in the same way, reheating the oil between batches. Strain the oil, and reheat it to 425°F/220°C. Add all the pork cubes, and deep-fry them for about 1 minute, turning constantly, until they are crisp and golden brown. Remove and drain thoroughly.

Remove the oil, reserving 2 tablespoons, and wipe out the wok. Heat the reserved oil until very hot. Stir-fry the green peppers and garlic for about 1 minute. Drain the marinated carrots and add them to the pan, together with the pineapple chunks. Stir-fry for another minute, and add the sauce. Heat the mixture, stirring constantly, until it begins to thicken. Add the pork cubes, and toss lightly to coat with the sauce. Serve immediately.

Serves 6

References

1 The Ideal Meat Producer

1 Charles Lamb, *The Works of Charles and Mary Lamb*, ed.
  E. V. Lucas (London, 1903), vol. II, pp. 123–4.
2 Jane and Michael Stern, *Two for the Road: Our Love Affair with
  American Food* (Boston, MA, 2006), p. 200.
3 Jane Grigson, *Charcuterie and French Pork Cookery* (London,
  1967), p. 10,

2 Prejudices Against the Pig

1 Maimonides, *The Guide for the Perplexed*, trans. Michael
  Friedländer, 2nd edn (London, 1919), part 3, ch. 48,
  pp. 370–71.
2 Fuchsia Dunlop, *Shark's Fin and Sichuan Pepper: A Sweet-sour
  Memoir of Eating in China* (New York, 2008), pp. 249–50.

3 Pork in Europe

1 Galen, *On the Properties of Foodstuffs*, trans. Owen Powell
  (Cambridge, 2003), p. 115.
2 Pliny the Elder, *Natural History*, Book 8, trans. Harris
  Rackham (Cambridge, MA, 1961), vol. III, p. 147.

3 Friedrich Engels, *The Condition of the Working Class in England*, trans. and ed. W. O. Henderson and W. H. Chaloner (Stanford, CA, 1968), p. 63.
4 E. B. White, *The Annotated Charlotte's Web*, notes by Peter F. Neumeyer (New York, 1994), p. 75.
5 William Cobbett, *Cottage Economy* (New York, 1970), p. 113.
6 Sidney cited in Alan Davidson, *The Oxford Companion to Food*, 2nd edn, ed. Tom Jaine (Oxford, 2006), p. 605.
7 Cobbett, *Cottage Economy*, pp. 103–6, 111, 117, 119–20.
8 *Household Words*, cited in Peter Simmonds, *The Curiosities of Food: or the Dainties and Delicacies of Different Nations* (Berkeley, CA, 2001), p. 3.
9 Alexis Soyer, *The Gastronomic Regenerator: A Simplified and Entirely New System of Cookery*, 8th edn (London, 1852), p. 202.
10 Alexis Soyer, *The Modern Housewife or Ménagère* (London, 1851), pp. 119, 198, 200.
11 Isabella Beeton, *Mrs Beeton's Book of Household Management*, enlarged edn (New York, 1986), pp. 362, 365.
12 Auguste Escoffier, *The Complete Guide to the Art of Modern Cookery*, trans. H. L. Cracknell and R. J. Kaufman (London, 1979), pp. 350, 352.

4 Pork in the New World

1 Cited in Waverley Root, *Food* (New York, 1980), p. 376.
2 Lyall Watson, *The Whole Hog* (Washington, DC, 2004), pp. 126–9.
3 Laura Ingalls Wilder, *Little House in the Big Woods* (New York, 1932), pp. 10–18.
4 William Cobbett, *Cottage Economy* (New York, 1970), pp. 112–13.
5 Cited in Richard Osborn Cummings, *The American and His Food* (Chicago, 1941), p. 12.
6 Cited in Susan Williams, *Food in the United States, 1820s–1890* (Westport, CT, 2006), p. 137.

7 Cited in Cummings, *The American and His Food*, p. 86.
8 Cited in D. C. McKeown, *Hog Wild* (New York, 1992),
   p. 97.
9 Michael Krondl, *Around the American Table* (Holbrook, MA,
   1995), p. 267.
10 Andrew F. Smith, ed., *The Oxford Encyclopedia of Food and
   Drink in America* (Oxford, 2004), vol. II, p. 492.
11 Frederick Douglass Opie, *Hog and Hominy: Soul Food from
   Africa to America* (New York, 2008), p. 32.
12 Mark Kurlansky, *The Food of a Younger Land: A Portrait of
   American Food . . . from the Lost WPA Files* (New York, 2009),
   pp. 147–55.
13 Opie, *Hog and Hominy*, pp. 42–3.
14 Cited in John Thorne and Matt Lewis Thorne, *Serious Pig:
   An American Cook in Search of His Roots* (New York, 1996),
   pp. 289–91.
15 Cited in Richard J. Hooker, *Food and Drink in America*
   (Indianapolis, IN, 1981), p. 221.
16 Cited in Megan J. Elias, *Food in the United States, 1890–1945*
   (Santa Barbara, CA, 2009), p. 15.
17 Eliza Leslie, *New Cookery Book* (Philadelphia, PA, 1857),
   p. 248
18 Sarah Josepha Hale, *The Good Housekeeper* [1841] (Mineola,
   NY, 1996), pp. 42–3; Fannie Merritt Farmer, *Boston Cooking-
   School Cookbook* [1896] (New York, 1997), pp. 208–9, 169.
19 Marion Cunningham, *The Fannie Farmer Cookbook*, 13th edn
   (New York, 1991), pp. 192, 198.
20 1816–17 and 1926–7 statistics from Cummings, *The
   American and His Food*, pp. 269–71. Statistics on meat consumption 1950–1994 from Richard L. Kohls and Joseph
   N. Uhl, *Marketing of Agricultural Products* (Upper Saddle
   River, NY, 1998), p. 399. Statistics for 2000 from Smith, ed.,
   Oxford Encyclopedia of Food and Drink in America, vol. II,
   p. 78.

5 Pork in the Far East

1 Jen Lin-Liu, *Serve the People: A Stir-fried Journey through China* (Orlando, FL, 2008), p. 33.
2 William Hedgepeth, *The Hog Book* [1978] (Athens, GA, 1998), p. 44.

6 Today's Mass-produced Pork

1 Isabella Beeton, *Mrs Beeton's Book of Household Management* (New York, 1986), pp. 364–5.
2 'Intensive Pig Farming', Wikipedia. See also the websites for Smithfield Foods, the National Pork Board, the Animal Welfare Institute and Niman Ranch.

Select Bibliography

Alford, Jeffrey, and Naomi Duguid, *Hot Sour Salty Sweet:*
    A Culinary Journey through Southeast Asia (New York, 2000)
Apicius, A Critical Edition, ed. Christopher Grocock and Sally
    Grainger (Totnes, 2006)
Beeton, Isabella, *Mrs Beeton's Book of Household Management,*
    enlarged edn (New York, 1986)
Cummings, Richard Osborn, *The American and His Food: History*
    of Food Habits in the United States, revised edn (Chicago, 1941)
Dalby, Andrew, and Sally Grainger, *The Classical Cookbook*
    (London, 1996)
Davidson, Alan, ed., *The Oxford Companion to Food,* 2nd edn, ed.
    Tom Jaine (Oxford, 2006)
Dunlop, Fuchsia, *Shark's Fin and Sichuan Pepper: A Sweet-sour*
    Memoir of Eating in China (New York, 2008)
Glasse, Hannah, *The Art of Cookery Made Plain and Easy*
    (London, 1983)
Grigson, Jane, *Charcuterie and French Pork Cookery* (London, 1967)
Hippisley-Coxe, Antony and Araminta, *Book of Sausages*
    (London, 1994)
Kaminsky, Peter, *Pig Perfect: Encounters with Remarkable Swine and*
    Some Great Ways to Cook Them (New York, 2005)
Lin-Liu, Jen, *Serve the People: A Stir-fried Journey through China*
    (Orlando, FL, 2008)
Opie, Frederick Douglass, *Hog and Hominy: Soul Food from Africa*
    to America (New York, 2008)

Smith, Andrew F., ed., *The Oxford Encyclopedia of Food and Drink in America* (Oxford 2004), 2 vols

Soyer, Alexis, *The Gastronomic Regenerator: A Simplified and Entirely New System of Cookery*, 8th edn (London, 1852)

—, *The Modern Housewife or Ménagère* (London, 1851)

Spencer, Colin, *British Food: An Extraordinary Thousand Years of History* (New York, 2002)

Thorne, John, with Matt Lewis Thorne, *Serious Pig: An American Cook in Search of His Roots* (New York, 1996)

Watson, Lyall, *The Whole Hog* (Washington, DC, 2004)

Websites and Associations

Pork Recipes

www.allrecipes.com (search under pork)

www.chinesefood.about.com (search under pork)

Pork Manufacturers

National Pork Board (US)
www.pork.org

Smithfield Foods
www.smithfieldfoods.com

Spam
www.spam.com

Humane Farming

Farm Sanctuary (US)
www.farmsanctuary.org

Humane Farming Association (US)
www.hfa.org

Niman Ranch (US)
www.nimanranch.com

Photo Acknowledgements

The author and the publishers wish to express their thanks to the below sources of illustrative material and/or permission to reproduce it:

Bigstock: pp. 31 (H. Brauer), 63 (ukrphoto), 64 (Marco Mayer), 74 (oysy), 89 (rafer); © The Trustees of the British Museum: pp. 48, 49; British Library: p. 35; Courtesy of Farm Sanctuary (farmsanctuary.org): p. 109; Istockphoto: pp. 34 (Linda Steward), 42 (dirkr), 52 (Robert Bremec), 65 (Siniša Botaš), 92 (Christian Baitg), 95 (Tupporn Sirichoo), 97 (Benjamin Loo), 98 (Tupporn Sirichoo), 102 (Michael Klee); Matthew W. Jackson: p. 76; Kunsthistoriches Museum, Wien: p. 39; Library of Congress: pp. 73, 79; Michael Leaman; pp. 18, 101; National Library of Medicine, Bethseda, Maryland: pp. 22, 40; Minneapolis College of Art and Design Collection: p. 53; Shutterstock: pp. 14, 32–3 (Foodpictures), 46 (Jiri Hera), 59 (Monkey Business Images), 94 (Hung Chung Chih), 106 (Iain Whitaker); Stockxchng: p. 105 (Chris Chidsey); Tate Gallery: p. 62; Peter G. Werner: p. 9.

Index

italic numbers refer to illustrations; **bold** to recipes